CHILD DEVELOPMENT
MORAL JUDGEMENT

CHILD DEVELOPMENT
MORAL JUDGEMENT

Chaya A. Heblikar

ANMOL PUBLICATIONS PVT. LTD.
NEW DELHI - 110 002 (INDIA)

ANMOL PUBLICATIONS PVT. LTD.
H.O.: 4374/4B, Ansari Road, Daryaganj,
New Delhi-110 002 (India)
Ph.: 23278000, 23261597
B.O.: No. 1015, Ist Main Road, BSK IIIrd Stage
IIIrd Phase, IIIrd Block,
Bangalore - 560 085 (India)
Visit us at: www.anmolpublications.com

Child Development: Moral Judgement

ISBN 978-81-261-3660-5

PRINTED IN INDIA

Printed at Mehra Offset Press, Delhi.

Dedicated
to My Guru

Swami
Chinmayananda

CONTENTS

ACKNOWLEDGEMENT

I wish to express my gratitude and heartfelt thanks to Prof. Dr. M. Khajapeer, Dean, Department of Education, Bangalore University, Bangalore for giving me an opportunity to undertake the present investigation.

I am also grateful to Dr. Talawar, Chairman, Department of Education, for his concern and encouragement.

I am deeply indebted to my guide Dr. Tara Sabapathy, Senior Lecturer, Department of Education, Bangalore University, Bangalore, for her valuable guidance and timely encouragement.

I thank the heads of the schools, the students and their parents of Bangalore City for their co-operation and help during the collection of data for this work.

I would also like to acknowledge the affection, help and consistent consideration shown to me by my husband Sri A.M. Heblikar, my little son, Sai Madhav, my mother-in-law, my mother, my family members and my friends, which enabled me to complete this work.

I also wish to express my special thanks to all those who have helped me in various ways.

LIST OF TABLES

CHAPTER I

INTRODUCTION

1.1. BACKGROUND OF THE STUDY

India has a rich cultural heritage of over five thousand years. The greatness of this culture is reflected in its religion. Indian religion contains the seeds of moral and spiritual values which are very necessary for the harmonious development of the individual. It is intimately bound up with the formation of character and the inculcation of ethical values. In ancient India, religious instruction formed a part of education which enabled the pupils in developing the right type of moral behaviour. The teachings of great religious teachers were a source of beacon light to the children which enabled them to develop the right kind of moral values, reflected in their moral behaviour.

It is clear that the moral behaviour of a child is conditioned by the religious moorings. It is more true in the case of a country like India, where religious tolerance is at its peak. Indian religion is the assimilation and synthesis of the good tenets of all other religions. Toynbee, the great English historian has stated that Indian religion is the mother of all religions and it teaches the need for good conduct, good moral behaviour and an upright life.

Moral behaviour has its root firmly fixed in tradition also. Tradition is the oral transmission of beliefs or practices from generation to generation. It is bound up with the continuity of family or community life. However blind traditional beliefs and prejudices should be discarded. Rabindranath Tagore says that, India should be free from dead thoughts and that we should not move in the narrow rut of caste prejudices and social barriers. But the finer feelings of love, sacrifice, honesty, truth and patriotism should be enthused in young children which improve their moral behaviour.

Moral behaviour is influenced by the society in which he lives since man is primarily a member of society. He is influenced by social organisations, such as family, peer group and community and social interactions that occur in them. There is also a close relationship between society and education. Culture guides the way of life of the members of a social group. Education transmits the culture of the community to its members. The common learned ways of living shared by the members of the society, consisting of the totality of tools, techniques, social institutions, attitudes, beliefs, motivations and systems of values known to the group tend to influence the moral behaviour. Man is always born into the environment of a culture and is placed within the customary social relationships. So, he is forcibly led to emulate proper behaviour. Society provides a cultural environment, which in turn influences moral behaviour. Man ultimately becomes the product of society. He becomes a decent man in a decent society.

1.2. MEANING OF MORALITY

Morality comes from the Latin word *moralis,* which means "customs, manners, or patterns of behaviour that conform to the standards of the group." According to Chave (1937),"... morality is the self-regulation of conduct with due consideration for both one's own welfare and the welfare of others. ... One cannot be moral until one recognises the social consequences of one's acts, and one is moral to the degree that one controls one's conduct with concern for these consequences... One may say that an act is right to the degree that it furthers the rights and the welfare of all those involved in the act and that it is wrong to the degree that it hinders the welfare and growth of anyone."

Morality is generally used to mean the accepted code of conduct in a society. It also means the pursuit of a good life. It is used in the sense of a condition with respect to discipline and confidence, pride, fixity of purpose and faith in the course espoused.

The individual has many potentialities of behaviour, he must choose between different courses of action. What he chooses will, in turn, determine the quality of his behaviour. And, in turn, this behaviour will be judged as right or wrong, depending upon what effect it has upon others.

When a person becomes morally "mature", his behaviour is regulated by controls from within himself, not by controls imposed upon him by his environment. A morally mature person, according to Wrenn (1949), is a "well disciplined person who has thorough control of himself, who takes care of the situation within himself and without outer regulation." His behaviour is characterised by increasing self-control, self-decision, and self-determination. However, he does not become a law unto himself. Instead, he takes into consideration the welfare of the group as well as of the different individuals who compose the group.

Every social group has its mores, or fundamental life philosophies, which are embodied in the morals and taboos of the group. These are the "shall" and "shall not" aspects of the culture of the group. In the case of a child, failure to do so is excused on the grounds that he does not understand or know the mores. But, by adolescence, the mores become rigidly binding, and any deviation from the approved pattern is met with a disapproval or punishment. Many of the mores are incorporated into law, with specific penalties attached for breaking of these laws (Landis, 1952).

The individual is judged by how he conforms or fails to conform to the standards of the group. These judgements lead society to label the individual as "moral" or "immoral", depending upon the degree of his conformity. From such judgements, the individual acquires a "reputation" in the group. The person who conforms to the dictates of the group not only wins a favourable reputation but also experiences satisfaction. Deviations from the group standards, on the other hand, lead to an unfavourable reputation and feelings of guilt. As Hollingworth (1949) has stressed, "many problems of adjustment in adolescence hinge on moral dilemmas. Improved insight into the meaning and origin of moral obligations may contribute effectively to attainment of happiness."

The individual learns to control his behaviour by conforming to the moral codes or moral "values" he has learned from the group. This learning takes place in three ways: through reward and punishment; through unconscious imitation of those with whom the individual is associated and whom he looks upon as his "ideal"; and through reflective thinking that results in generalised moral principles to apply to situations that may arise in the future and that are similar to the one in which the moral principle was formed (Havighurst and Taba, 1949).

Moral training consists not only of teaching the individual the moral codes of the group but also of instilling in him a high regard for these codes, so that he will be willing to accept them and guide his behaviour accordingly. Many adolescents, as is true of children and adults, know what is considered right, but they may, for one reason or another, refuse to accept this standard as their own. Only fear of punishment or loss of social esteem motivates them to conform to a moral standard they refused to accept. When, therefore, there is the possibility of escaping punishment or loss of social approval, they act in accordance with their own standards, disregarding the standards of the group. The individual who, by contrast, accepts the moral standards of the group controls his own behaviour, thus making external restraints unnecessary.

As the social horizons broaden in adolescence, the individual is faced with inconsistencies in moral values in much the same manner as he is faced with inconsistencies in religious values. No longer do the moral values learned in the narrow environment of his childhood days apply to all the new social groups in the school, neighbourhood, and community with which he affiliates himself. He discovers variations according to socio-economic status, sex, national origin, and many other factors. This, combined with the greater sensitivity to inconsistency that results from his higher value of intelligence, causes confusion, which not only complicates the learning of moral values appropriate for his level of development but which also has a marked influence on his behaviour.

The adolescent of today is faced with more moral alternatives than members of the older generations ever had to face. This is due to many causes, the most important of which are: (a) movement in modern society, which results in the adolescent's leaving the neighbourhood and family group early in life; (b) rapid change in all phases of life, which has resulted in the breakdown of well-established moral standards, with the result that parents lack positiveness in their teaching of moral precepts or they neglect it entirely; and (c) adolescent codes holding sway in many of the youth groups, with little chaperonage by adult codes (Landis, 1952). When the moral values of the adolescent's peer group differs markedly from those of his parents, the parents refuse to accept these new moral values, with the result that there is constant friction between the adolescent and his parents (Kuhlen, 1952).

In meeting the problem of conflicting moral values, the adolescent must first know what values to accept and then have sufficient experience in meeting such conflicts, so that he will be able to do so when he is independent of adult guidance and help. The role of parents and teachers is very crucial at this stage of moral development of adolescents. They must therefore pay special attention during this period.

Indian Concept of Morality

The Indian concept of morality is based on the idea of *dharma* (duty). *Sathyam vada Dharmam chara* (Tell the truth, do the duty) – These two sterling qualities enunciated the tenets of morality. *Dharma* means to uphold certain noble things in life. If we protect *dharma*, it protects us. *Dharma* forms an important part of life. We must uphold certain principles in life. Morality is one of them. Protection and progress are the constituents of *dharma*. One who follows *dharma* must be duty-conscious.

Dharma means nature. It is that which is inherent and cannot be given up or taken on. Our own true nature is *Sat-Cit-Ananda* (Existence-Consciousness-Bliss). To abide in one's own nature is called following *swadharma*. *Swadharma* is the individual's tendencies and *vasanas* with which one has come into the world to exist. That which determines one man's personality as distinctly different from another is his thoughts which are in turn determined by his *vasanas*. To act against the grain of one's own *vasanas* is to act in terms of *paradharma*. Following *paradharma* brings sorrow and is fraught with fear (*paradharmo bhayaavahah – Geeta,* Ch. 3). Since the Divine Self is the true nature of man and since the Self is Eternal, the Hindu *Dharma* which deals with it is called as the Eternal *dharma* or *Sanatana dharma*. That which remains in a substance from the beginning to the end constantly and which is its most essential property is called its *dharma*. For example: sapidity in liquids, heat and light in the sun, sweetness in sugar are the essential properties of the very *dharma* in them.

The most essential factor in man is *atman*, the Touch of Life. Therefore the essential *dharma* of man is the Divine Spark of Existence, the Infinite Lord. *dharma* not only indicates all the ethical and moral rules of conduct, all duties in life, all duties towards relations, friends, community, nation and the world, all our obligations to our environment, all our affections, reverence, charity and sense of goodwill in and through our physical, mental and intellectual actions, but in addition to live truly as the *atman*, and to express its Infinite Perfection through all our actions and in all our contacts with the world outside is to bring forth expression of one's true *dharma* and to rediscover our *dharma*.

One should practice dharmic rites which will form moral rites. Ramakrishna Paramahamsa and his disciple Vivekananda have given special preference to *dharma* which will lead to moral values. When a person dies, only his dharmic acts follow him. Non-violence is the essence of *dharma*. We should not harm any living object in this world. Basavanna says that *dharma* includes kindness, which leads to a moral behaviour. This is one of the qualities of moral behaviour and morality, according to the Indian concept.

Everyone should follow the tenets of his *dharma* which has been handed down to him from generation to generation. We should not hate the different *dharma*s followed by others. At the same time, we should not discard our *dharma*. The Indian Constitution does not interfere with the private life of its citizens in the matter of *dharma*. *Dharma* which means 'duty', in its broad sense should be followed according to what is known as Varnashrama *dharma*. The Indian concept of morality stresses the importance of moral and ethical values.

Ancient Indian system of education attached great importance to the ethical pursuits. Character training was given the main prominence. Character, conduct and behaviour were considered as the primary qualities of morality. According to the Indian concept of morality education must lead the youth to the things that are true, honest, pure, lovely, and of good report. Formation of right conduct is character developing process. This ultimately leads to moral development. A child develops moral force and as a result becomes highly moral.

1.3. MORAL JUDGEMENT

Moral judgement is a by-product of the child's general social experience. Patterning of experience is necessary before the child is capable of higher forms of moral judgement. The ability to make moral judgement plays an important role in the moral development, as it is a process of defining a happening in terms of moral justifiability. It is the insight to see the relationship between an abstract principle and concrete cases. It is the cognitive capacity which helps the child to evaluate the worthiness or unworthiness of an action. It requires the ability to look for the common features of apparently different situations and to evaluate the situation as right or wrong.

Moral judgement made by individuals is related to the level and kind of intellectual process of which they are capable. Moral judgements are judgements about the good and right action. Not all judgements of good or right are moral judgements. However, many are judgements of authentic, provential or technological goodness or rightness.

Moral judgement is the result of a complex and interactive process of many psychological, social, cognitive and emotional factors. It is a by product of many other learning. It is made up of self control, awareness of self, skill and insight reaction to authority of parents and of cultural mores. A large part of that mature balance of judgement which sees individual rights in clear perspective with the rights of others and the relationship of one's own present behaviour to one's own future well being is called moral judgement.

Piaget and his followers have identified different types of moral judgements which appeared in children of different age groups.

Types of Moral Judgement

1. Intentionality in moral judgement

Young children judge an act in terms of its actual physical consequences where as older children judge in terms of the intent of the person.

2. Relativities in judgement

The young child sees acts as either totally right or totally wrong and believes that everyone viewed them in the same way. The older child on the other hand is aware of a diversity of views of right and wrong.

3. Independence of actions

For the young child an act is bad if it elicits punishment, while the older child says an act is bad because it violated a rule and does harm to others.

4. Use of reciprocity

Young children show selfish and concrete reciprocity in their judgements and say, "hit him back". They anticipate relation and returns of favour equally from others while older children judge in terms of sentiments of gratitude from past affections and favours shown by others.

5. The use of punishment as a restitution and reform

Young children sanction severe and arbitrary punishment of misdeeds, where as older children increasingly favour milder punishment as well on the acts of restitution to the victim and reform of the culprit.

6. Naturalistic view of misfortune

Young children view accidents and misfortunes occurring after misdeeds as punishments willed by a deity, God or nature, older children do not interpret accidents and natural misfortunes as punishment or misdeeds.

One of the increasingly important tasks of education is to help children to develop the appropriate skills and judgement to cope up with the variety of moral choices they have to face in today's complex world. Moral judgement in the present study is defined in terms of five dimensions namely, Honesty, Truthfulness, Non-Violence, Obedience and Justice.

Dimensions of Moral Judgement

Honesty

Values are the essence of morality handed down by each human generation to the succeeding generation for its well being. Values are essential in order to establish and maintain peace among human race and lead it to further progress. Values help to evolve codes for the right kind of human behaviour. These are normally expressed in the form of moral codes such as 'Honesty is the best policy'. The will to take up to the challenges that one comes across in the world is born out of one's own courage of conviction. Everyone of us has ideas of our own but only a few live up to them. At the mere suggestion of a challenge to those ideals, we readily tend to fall a victim to it and become ready to compromise with our ideals. This is dishonest living. So honesty is a strong will and the ability to live up to the intellectual convictions and to act thereafter in terms of that knowledge.

Honesty is the beginning point of all ethical behaviour – one can not be ethical without being honest. When we leave honesty out of ethics we get hypocrisy, an insidious and pervasive form of dishonesty. Young people can not learn human values when the actions of their parents and leaders in society contradict their practice. Hypocrisy thrives when being ethical is equated with being nice. One often gains advantages by agreeing with all sides and tabling one's own convictions about values. The only antidote is to have courage and the ability to take the alternative course following the two continuing obligations: i.e., to benefit others, and to do no harm to others. Good begets good, no matter what the reason for doing it. It is the law of the universe: each thing creates its kind. A continuing erosion that attacks the full range of human values in a society can not withstand for long the courage of honest people however few in number.

How one can get this courage and honesty of one's convictions is a matter of living life itself in a manner far too different than it is generally held by people. History stands testimony of the life and events of Living Saviours in the world who provided such examples and taught men the ways of righteous living. *Satya, dharma, shanti, prema* and *ahimsa* are such value guidelines that transcend all culturally held notions. Having goodness is not nearly so easy nor so culturally acceptable as having religion and therefore value standards, although common to all major religions, need not be necessarily contingent upon a belief in any of them as traditionally held. Ethical values precede and lead to law. The ethics that is embodied into the law is usually based on the morality of the majority. When the morality of the majority operates at a lower level than the law, it requires great courage for someone to set the trend in the right direction.

According to Gandhiji honesty is in his refusing to copy from the neighbour's book, repentance for sin by acknowledging his faults in his confession to his father, keeping up his promises of not touching meat, wine and woman. Thus honesty is a social obligation. An individual should be honest to his people at home or in the family, to all those he comes across in the school or office, etc. he should also be honest to the state in which he lives. A statesman should display his honesty in dealing with national and international issues or problems.

An individual may have to face many problems and difficulties in living an honest life. He may have to incur the displeasure or even enmity of his own kith and kin, his superiors or colleagues or others. The consequences may be serious. Should one give up the moral stand of being honest because of adverse circumstances? 'Is not putting duty first, and success second, a way of raising the standard of virtue? says Confucius.

There may be temptations of many kinds from different sources to induce an individual to go against his conscience. To overcome such temptations, the agent should have the will power, a firm faith that he would succeed at all costs in his endeavour, and a determination not to yield to threat or temptation. Sometimes an apparently just cause may be put forth to change his stand which may commit him to a dishonest act. The result in the process may appear to be attractive and to be benefiting many. Even then one should bear in mind that means are as important as the ends. An honest person will not try to justify his dishonest means in achieving something worthwhile. To remember the Chinese philosopher Confucius when he said, "It may be possible to seize and carry off the chief commander of a large army, but not possible so to rob one poor fellow of his will."

Truthfulness

Truth is the basis of *dharma,* and *dharma* is indestructible. So truth and *dharma* are unchangeable by human connivance or convenience. The true interpretation of *dharma* is to ask for the well-being of the entire human community, where there is no place for selfishness, pride of power and pelf, and envy; where wars may be waged but only for the protection of rights of others and not for self-aggrandisement. According to Gandhiji, truth is the sovereign principle which includes numerous other principles. This truth is not only truthfulness in words but truthfulness in thought also, and not only the relative truth of our conception, but the absolute truth, the eternal principle, that is God. He also said that truth is as old as the hills. But some ethical theorists hold that truth is an intrinsic value to man, that is, it is a value by itself.

According to Swami Vivekananda one gets truth from both microcosm and macrocosm world by experience and by experimentation. Psychology, Metaphysics and Religion are concerned with the microcosm. The physical and the biological sciences are concerned with the macrocosm. A perfect truth should be in harmony with experiences in both these worlds.

The human intellect alone can keep up certain fundamental values or ideals in its understanding and act up to them. The secret of success in life lies in keeping the head above the storms of the heart. At the intellectual level, one must be ready to consider and reconsider for a thousand times, and in the light of all the evidences available, one must be ready to accept or reject an idea or an ideal. But having once accepted an ideal, one must discover in himself the heroism to live up to it always. This is called Truthfulness. This is the spring- source of the will and courage to act and achieve.

Non-violence

Shakespeare has beautifully expressed this idea of non-violence in his Hamlet, 'I am cruel only to be kind'. For example, a surgeon may appear cruel and bloody, while performing surgery, but his heart means well. Such actions, though physically hurting and causing pain, would fall under *ahimsa* or non-violence.

Kripalani says, 'Prophets and seers generally enlarge or deepen the scope and application of the laws that already exist. He illustrates this point by what Jesus Christ did to the law, ' an eye for an eye and a tooth for a tooth,' given by Moses to the Jews; Moses had emphasised that revenge and retaliation should not exceed the original injury. Christ said, 'Bless them that curse you, do good to them that hate you, Gandhiji simply carried forward and enhanced the law of non-violence preached by Buddha, Mahavira, Christ and other Prophets. According to him there is a necessity of Self-purification as a pre-condition for practising *ahimsa.*

'Mentally don't injure others' is the creed of *ahimsa*. The teachers of Hinduism commended this eternal value of life, *'ahimsa'* to be lived at the mental level meaning mentally never curse anyone, never wish harm to any body. Non-violence does not mean 'non-killing' or 'non-injury' at the physical level. Sometimes we may have to be cruel and injurious externally even though the heart behind our actions is full of love and kindness.

In a community, if they have no concept of non-violence to the other communities, there will not be any peace between the communities in the world. Whenever these values are lived for generation, whether at the individual level, or at the communal level or at the national level, we shall certainly find that there is a greater blaze of joy and peace, love and serenity in the society. The generations that decide to understand and live these values, they in their harmonious strength become morally strong and healthier, not only to face tragedies of their own times, but healthier also to enjoy the peace and tranquility of their historical era.

Obedience

Obedience is an essential quality to be cultivated by all especially by the younger generation that are the leaders in the making. Because the popular saying goes that "one who knows to obey alone knows to command also." The term obedience is used in connection with an individual's relationship with – a) parents at the family level, b) teachers at the level of the educational institutions, c) superiors at the occupational level and d) teachers chosen by the individual for self-improvement at the social and religious level. All these denote people who possess one or more of the following qualifications and standing, like higher level of maturity and wisdom, educational qualification, achievements in the world, seniority in age or people with natural love and affection and well wishers.

Obedience makes one mature and imparts discipline, wisdom, education and good behaviour thereby making the individual a better person in the society. Obedience develops respect for the person in command. It also gives humility, which in turn is the beginning of learning in any field. Obedience also gives the ability to live and work in harmony with others, which is the most important quality for success in any endeavour. Obedience is a quality, which breeds all the above positive qualities, and it certainly should not be taken for meet passive acceptance, which curbs original thinking. A person who knows to obey cheerfully and with cooperation to the best of his capacity even when commands are not to his liking or not practical to his judgement shines better when he is in a position to command, for the experience teaches him to handle the situations more diligently.

Justice

History is full of information about the Kings and Kingdoms, which flourished and reached heights of glory and wealth where justice prevailed and there is no dearth for illustrations of downfall of people and society where justice failed. Justice is the healthy offshoot of Truthfulness and Integrity.

It is essential to be justful at the individual level first. It helps in developing the individual's integrity and thereby makes him achieve his goal and prosperity. After all each one strives to get his share and improve his position in the society constantly. In the process lack of proper direction and value education prompts the individual to adopt shortcut methods of being unjust and obtaining prosperity. People even have gone to the extent of saying that one cannot get anything in this world if one adheres to justice. But little do the individuals who have taken to the short cut methods realize that what they achieve that way gives them temporary gain. They lose their integrity-giving raise to a split personality and ultimately loss of their mental serenity and health. Such individuals when increases in number the society itself loses its harmony and there is injustice violence and unrest every where which marks the downfall of that society and culture. The result is that the people who have material wealth suffer for want of security and the people who lack the same also suffer for want of means for their existence.

If the student community who are the leaders of tomorrow are caught when they are young and made to understand the value of truthfulness, honesty and accommodation, justice will automatically follow, because justice flows from higher level to the lower. When the governing bodies at all level are integrated and just, the era turns to be a golden era.

Thus the five dimensions of moral judgement indicate the extent an individual is capable of judging the behaviour of himself and of others in terms of moral and ethical expectation within the society.

1.4. MORAL DEVELOPMENT

Work of Jean Piaget (1965)

Piaget's main aim was to explore the nature of children's moral judgements and, to do this, he worked in Geneva with individual children, talking to them and questioning them on three broad areas: their attitudes to rules; their judgements of rights and wrong; and their assessment of justice and fairness. He established that growth in moral judgement is a gradual developmental process, involving not the learning of rules by rewards, punishment or imitation, but rather a progress of cognitive restructuring.

In 1932 Piaget wrote that, "all morality consists in a system of rules and the essence of all morality is to be sought for in this respect which the individual acquires for those rules." In view of this, then, one of the crucial questions for Piaget was how the young child's mind comes to understand and respect rules. He was concerned not only with the child's practice of rules (his moral conduct) but also with the way in which the child perceives rules as a restraint on his actions. For his investigations Piaget chose rules children follow in playing the game of marbles (universally popular among the child population of Geneva at that time), since this kind of rule is one seldom passed on by adults but learnt from other children during the game itself. He himself joined in their games adopting the position of one ignorant of the rules and conventions, and in conversation with children, discovered how their approach to rules changes as they mature.

The very youngest children play haphazardly with no regard for rules at all, but later, upto the age of about six, they become more and more aware of the rules of the game, now regarding them as immutable and following them rigidly. This reflects the child's heteronomy, obeying rules laid down for him externally which are not to be questioned. But later he gradually begins to realise that rules are not sacrosanct and have been formulated in order to regulate the game. Rather than being untouchable they can be modified by mutual agreement with the other players. It is during this stage that heteronomy begins to give way to autonomy and around the age of eleven or twelve children begin to show an interest in how and why rules are formulated. They are not now concerned with putting them rigidly into practice, but are ready to modify them by mutual agreement according to circumstance.

In Piaget's view, one of the main factors contributing towards this developing autonomy is the child's growing ability to cooperate with others. Where rules were seen, at an earlier stage, as emanating from some authority figure, respect for them was unilateral rather than mutual. It is only when children experience relationships with their peers, meeting together as equals, that the opportunity arises for mutual consent and cooperation and the scene is set for the growth of autonomy. But in order to move towards autonomy it seems essential for the child to be released from constraints imposed by authority figures where adults use their superior force. Cooperative activities and mutual understanding between peers are, in Piaget's view, necessary conditions for autonomy to develop.

An examination of some of Piaget's work on children's judgements of right and wrong, indicates a gradual progression from a stage of heteronomy to one of autonomy. Actions are at first regarded by young children as right if an adult approves of them, wrong if he disapproves. Children at the heteronomous stage judge conduct according to its material consequences, rather than the intentions behind the act.

To explore children's judgements of rights and wrong Piaget used a story technique, presenting the children with pairs of incidents and asking them to comment on the behaviour of the characters portrayed. For example, children were asked whether a girl who accidentally cut a large hole in her dress when she was trying to help her mother with some dressmaking was naughtier than a child who deliberately played with scissors when she had been told not to and made a small snip in her dress. Younger children almost without exception judged the first case as more severe and more deserving of punishment: the act was judged as naughtier because the girl made a bigger hole. Piaget terms this stage in the formation of moral judgements "moral realism"; the child is forming his judgement on the basis of what he can observe happening around him in his reality, that is, on material consequences. Similarly, on hearing stories about a boy who stole a roll to give to a hungry friend and a girl who stole a piece of ribbon, judgements were made on the basis of the cost of the stolen article – that which was immediate and real to the child.

This tendency of young children to focus on external, observed consequences of actions and to ignore intentions can be explained by reference to the child's egocentricity. In Piaget's stage theory of cognitive growth, a child at the egocentric level is still limited in his ability to distinguish himself and his own feelings from those of others. He is capable of seeing things only from his own point of view, does not always distinguish fact from fantasy (dreams, to him, are real) and thus cannot conceive that other viewpoints are possible. He cannot internalise rules and apply them to actions in a flexible enough manner to take into account factors which might be variable: for example, other people's intentions or the different demands made by varying circumstances. It is only as he emerges from this state of egocentricity and begins to be able to focus on more than one aspect of a situation at a time, and, in particular, on unobservable, aspects, that his moral judgements become more flexible. Thus an older child, confronted with the anecdotes about stealing, might argue that whereas it is usually wrong to steal, it is not so bad if your friend is starving. Consideration for others is now assuming an important part in a child's life, as a result, Piaget argues, a peer group cooperation and interaction.

It is this development of mutual respect that enables a child to begin to see the world through other people's eyes. It is only when he can consider all possible circumstances and points of view before making a moral judgement, one that fits a particular set of circumstances, that he can truly be said to have reached a stage of autonomy or to practise a rational moral code instead of being tied to a conventional morality.

Hence Piaget recognises two types of morality in childhood – one is heteronomous morality, which is authoritarian moral code imposed upon the child; the other is autonomous morality, which is rational and democratic, and arises from the interaction between the child and his peers. Morality develops from the heteronomy to autonomy.

In summary, then, Piaget distinguishes between two kinds of morality. Conventional morality is reflected in an obedience to adult command and an uncritical adherence to rules. This is described as a stage of moral realism or heteronomy, characterised by unilateral respect for and dependence upon others for guidance in moral issues. Rational morality is reached where children are able to formulate their own moral rules by mutual agreement and to apply them according to circumstance rather than rigidly and immutable.

Children do not practise either conventional or rational morality to the exclusion of the other, but move from one to another by a process of maturation, development and cognitive restructuring. Thus Piaget assumes that a child's development in moral judgements is paralleled by his cognitive development in other spheres. A stage theory of development is thus postulated with the observation that children pass through stages in an invariant order even though not all at the same rate. Some do not ever attain the final stage of absolute autonomy.

A stage theory of development is characterized by several unique features. Firstly the concept "stage" supercedes that of chronological or mental age and although it is possible to say, for example, that children do not begin to emerge from the stage of heteronomy until about the age of eleven or twelve, it must be remembered that age is only a very rough guide. Children do not all develop at the same rate, so some will progress more rapidly through the stages than others. Secondly, the sequence of stages has been demonstrated as being invariant: it is not possible either to miss out a stage or to pass through them in a different order, though exceptional children, as Williams and Williams (1969) have shown, will show flashes of insight characteristic of an advanced stage long before they are firmly established in that stage. Thirdly, progression from one stage to another does not involve simply an addition to what went before but, implies a reorganisation or restructuring, enabling the child to see problems and thus to make moral judgements from a different and more complex perspective. Fourthly, the concept of stages should not be taken in a literal or chronological sense. All adults will respond to some situations in a heteronomous manner.

The great value of Piaget's work on moral judgements lies both in the methods he used to investigate children's thought process and in the fact that he was the first to view moral thought as a developmental and restructuring process depending largely on a child's growth towards abstract thinking and interaction with his environment and with those with whom he comes into contact.

Jean Piaget in his book, "The Origin of Intelligence in Children," has dealt with the different stages of the development of child's moral judgement. Development of child's moral judgement takes place mainly in four stages. They are:

1. Moral development within the family

A child's moral development passes through various succeeding stage. This moral development is more than mental, emotional and social development. Approbation or rejection of the various activities of the child takes place at home by the parents. The parents accept the good actions and reject bad actions, of the child at home. The child judges its action as bad or wrong when parents disapproves or criticise it. Similarly all actions, which are approved and welcomed by parents will be construed as good and correct by child. Reward or punishment will act as a contributory factor for the child's moral judgement. Further the moral development of the child depends on his emotional development also. To reward for an action brings satisfaction and happiness to the child. The child considers such an action as right and correct. On the other hand when the action of the child meets with punishment, the child realises that his action is morally wrong and incorrect. Thus the child develops the moral judgement of his action within the family. He forms the concepts of good and bad in this way. But his concepts depending upon his parental ideas may not always be correct. In a family, the parents may think that the mixing of boys and girls is incorrect. Then the child will think that such an action is wrong. But if in certain families such a thing is not objected to, the child will develop a similar kind of moral judgement. This kind of development of moral concept in his infancy by the child may continue for long in his childhood also.

2. Moral development in school and neighbourhood

As the child grows into a boy, he enters in to the neighbourhood in search of suitable companions for play. Then his companions influence him with regard to the concept of good and bad. He adopts the ethos of the group, as he will have become a member. He welcomes as correct what the group does and denounces such things as the group rejects. He may be so much influenced by the group morality and behaviour that he may unlearn that he has formerly learnt at home. There is bound to be inconsistency in the boy's conduct at this stage. His moral conduct now may not confirm to the moral conduct at home. Circumstances will guide him in judging certain moral conducts right or wrong. Under certain peculiar and exceptional circumstances he may justify such act of immorality. Therefore the propriety of his moral behaviour differs as he learns through the school of life. He will develop desires and prejudices by his association with the group.

In his school life, a child may follow his seniors in concluding certain moral judgement. Then it becomes a pattern for conduct and behaviour. This only shows that parents and teachers are largely responsible, for developing the right kind of moral judgement in their wards. No doubt, an individual's moral judgement is influenced by laws, traditions, religious ideals, customs and systems. But this is not always the case. There may be exceptions. An individual may not always accept the general concept of propriety. The moral development of the child at this stage becomes a complex process, a process of action and interaction of an individual. In many cases, the child may choose his own criterion however rudimentary it may be and form his own moral judgement.

3. Moral development during adolescence

Adolescence is the most crucial stage in the life of an individual. The moral development at this stage is crucial. The youth will be susceptible to the effects of his mental and social development. At this stage, the sexual urge will be particularly intense for both male and female adolescents. It is only natural therefore that the ideas of good and bad will be associated with sexual behaviour. The laws of sexual behaviour differ considerably in various cultures. There is no universal law exhibited regarding the moral concepts and conduct of adolescents at this stage. They differ according to their culture. At this stage, sexual education will have most profitable influence upon the adolescent's moral development and judgement. Instead of suppression of sexual instincts, it is desirable to inculcate sublimation and modification. Moral and ethical teaching should be imparted through practical representation of best ideas and values. Academic teachings and preaching will be of no avail. It is equally necessary that teachers and parents set the best example. At the same time the school atmosphere must be made congenial for the moral development of the students.

4. Influence of Society and Culture

Moral development of the individuals is also influenced by the general social atmosphere. This is the reason why moral behaviour and conduct of individuals belonging to cultured and uncivilised societies show marked differences. They are almost incompatible. An individual's concepts are formed in society. The general morality existing in society is generally accepted by the multitude. Individuals like leaders, scientists, reformers, rectors and literatures influence the moral development of the individual.

There are indirect matters which influence moral judgement of the individual. They are life situations such as employment or unemployment, inability to secure the desired profession, economic status of the family, atmosphere in the family and the intellectual and social status. Friends also influence the moral development and judgement of an individual. In this connection it may be stated rightly that a man is known by the company he keeps. Moral level of friends and classmates wield an influence on the moral development of an individual.

Moral development varies with individuals. Generally speaking we may say that good situations normally have a desirable influence. Varying stages of moral judgement in the child and varying levels of judgement in the adult both reflect differences in shaping moral concepts. These vary from one individual to another and these variable factors must be taken into account while seeking to trace the development. The key variables are relationships at home concerning the parental behaviour, value and child practices. All such factors are involved in the moral development. Thus it could be seen that moral judgement is a blanket term covering a number of related factors.

The Work of Kohlberg (1966)

Besides Piaget's work, Kohlberg's can probably be said to have made the most important contribution to the psychology of moral development. Kohlberg, working in the USA, has in his empirical research both complemented and expanded Piaget's ideas. Like Piaget, he too concentrates largely on individuals moral judgement; that is, the reasoning behind the judgements they make, rather than their actual moral conduct. Kohlberg (1966) too adopts a cognitive theory of moral development and sets out to show that principles of moral judgement gradually develop as children grow older, but that this development is highly dependent on environmental and social conditions. His conviction that external influences can foster children's moral thinking and help them to move onto a further more complex stage leads to offer a framework for practical moral education.

Kohlberg's scheme of moral development takes the form of six main stages, each of which reveals a different kind of motivation for acting morally or for forming moral judgements.

Stage 1: Punishment and Obedience Orientation

At stage 1 of the premoral level, we find that an individual's motives are oriented primarily towards obedience and punishment. A child at this stage will say that it is wrong to disobey his father because he will be found out and punished or that he must not, for instance, run across the road because his father has said so. Conformity is largely a function to avoid punishment. A child obeys rules only to avoid punishment. Gradually this is abandoned for stage 2.

Stage 2: Naive Instrumental Hedonism

At stage 2, the actions which are regarded as morally right are those which satisfy the individual's needs. A child behaves morally so as to obtain rewards to have his own favours returned. The child in this case is egocentrically oriented.

Stage 3: Interpersonal Concordance

The child confirms to avoid disapproval or being disliked. The child adopts a good boy, nice girl concept. Moral behaviour at this stage is good behaviour that pleases others. It can be considered a morality of social reinforcement.

Stage 4: Law and Order Orientation

Conformity appears out of respect for authorities and preservations of the social order. Here the behaviour is motivated by the desire to avoid guilt that may occur if one is detected in the violation of acknowledged and accepted rights and duties. Stages 3 and 4, at the level of what Kohlberg calls conventional role conformity, represent firstly, the "good boy" orientation where the child's actions and judgements are made in order to gain approval from others, while later (at stage 4) this gives way to a respect of authority and the given social order. A child will, for example, conform to avoid censure from an authority figure.

Stage 5: Social Contact – Legalistic Orientation

A person considers his contact with others as a morally binding matter. Moral action is viewed in relation to individuals rights of standards for behaviour that have been achieved by critical discussion and consensus with society. In a primitive society, the judgement is given by the *panchayat.* They critically discuss and based on the total conscience the punishment is given. The type of punishment is also judged by the *panchayat.*

Stage 6: Universal Ethical Principle Orientation

At this most advanced stage, abstract and ethical principles are taken as indication of universal morality. The moral values are considered as 'self chosen' and the individual makes selection of principles to guide this behaviour. It is not until the individual reaches stages five and six at the level of self-accepted moral principles that he begins to approach what Kohlberg considers to be moral maturity. At stage five the rights of others are considered and an effort is made to see that these rights are respected and safeguarded. It is rather more a contractual orientation than one involving any feeling for the position of others. At the final stage, probably not attained by the majority of the population, the morally mature person acts according to his own conscience or principles. He is now able to consider universal values involving the rights and feelings of others and his own behaviour towards them.

On the basis of this analysis, Kohlberg maintains that –

1. These levels and stages of moral development are strongly cognitively determined.
2. Each is a unique emergence from the preceding one and is qualitatively different.
3. The six sequences are invariance and travel from 1st to 6th.
4. The development of the process is similar to all culture.
5. A greater consistency between one's moral belief and his actual behaviour in situations involving moral conflict will occur at higher stages of development.
6. Moral development is irreversible.
7. Each stage is unitary, i.e., in all areas of morality the individual will judge and tend to behave according to the general principles or belief of that stage.

As in any stage concept, the order of the stages is regarded as invariant; an individual can neither miss out a stage nor take them in a different order. And for Kohlberg, this invariance goes further to include universality under different cultural conditions. This does not mean that in any culture, movement through the stages proceeds at the same rate, but rather that the sequence is the same and that, regardless of the nature of the culture, all stages emerge, with the possible exception of the last. Kohlberg's own cross-cultural studies of moral development (1966) compared the moral judgements made by ten to sixteen year olds in Taiwan (urban population), in a Malaysian aboriginal tribal village, and in a Turkish village, with those made by an American sample. The findings suggest a similar sequence of development in all culture, although stages 5 and 6 do not develop clearly in preliterate communities.

Kohlberg (1966) also established that subcultural difference occur, not in basic moral values but in rate of progress through the stages. At all ages middle-class children tended to be somewhat in advance of their working-class peers. This he attributed to a difference in children's feelings of their participation in a prevailing social order and in their understanding of it. If working-class children find themselves in an authoritarian family set-up (though obviously not all working-class families are of this type) then their individual value as persons is accorded less importance than their position in the family. It would follow then that their moral orientations would lean further towards gaining the approval of others and avoiding censure (stages three and four) than towards a personal autonomous stance as in stages 5 and 6.

Kohlberg's stage theory, like Piaget's implies a cognitive restructuring and reordering as the individual matures morally. Each stage of development allows a better and more complex cognitive grasp than the one before it; elements of earlier stages are taken into account of but are transformed in the light of later understanding and more complex mental structures. Kohlberg attempts to explain how individuals pass from one stage to the next by drawing on the notion of cognitive conflict and introduces the "one stage above" principle. His thesis is that when children are presented with arguments one stage above the level they have reached, the conflict or mismatch in the arguments will prompt them to attempt a resolution of the problem and thus help them towards the next stage of moral argument.

Although Kohlberg sets out a developmental sequence, showing how children's moral judgements develop and mature as they pass from a premoral level to one where they are capable of making mature moral judgements, his pattern does not only offer an explanation of the child's moral thinking. In addition it goes some way towards furnishing a theory of moral character, suggesting an explanation of individual differences in the moral nature of adults. As we have already mentioned, not everyone reaches the final stage of moral maturity and many of us do not appear to have progressed at all from stage one, like those who simply conform to certain standards set up by others because of fear of punishment. If punishment is unlikely, that is, if there is minimal risk of their being found out in their infringement of rules, they have no hesitation in doing just as they like – no inner moral principle appears to operate. Adults are then to be found at any stage, and from this we are able to talk of a character type, if a person's conduct and quality of moral judgement are consistent.

Although research in this area is still in its early stage, findings suggest that it might be possible to account for an individual's fixation at an early stage and therefore, upto a point, for his moral character, by exploring other aspects of his social and moral life. Haan *et al.* (1968), working with college students, found that relatively few came out at the level of self-accepted moral principles on Kohlberg's scale of moral judgements. Those who did were found to be highly independent of their parents, to play an active part in social and political organisations, and to rely very little on religious doctrines for moral guidance, a point which may provide additional support. Those who came out at the level of conventional morality tended to be generally conservative, to play little part in social or political activities, and to conform to conventional standards set by parents and other authority figures.

Work of Norman J. Bull (1965)

The question whether one's moral action can be trusted to be based on one's capacity for moral judgement is raised by Norman J. Bull and he candidly admits that there could be no relation between one's moral judgement and his conduct. However he says, 'yet it remains true that the moral knowledge and understanding are pre-requisites of moral action' and so he pursues his study of moral development in children.

Whereas Piaget has identified only two distinctly different stages of moral development in children, Norman J. Bull has recognised four stages of moral development. They are Anomy, Heteronomy, Socionomy and Autonomy. These stages are in the order of chronological age development of the child. However, each stage seems to overlap its succeeding stages to some extent. But each stage has its own characteristic features. Below are given the more important characteristics of each of these stages.

Anomy

This is the stage of morality from birth upto a few years of childhood. This being the earlier stage the child has not developed any sense of morality or immorality. It is so to say amoral with no capacity for moral judgement. The behaviour of the child is based purely on his instincts and controlled by pleasure or pain as a result of natural consequences. So long as the child does not receive any training and does not have opportunities to see examples of good moral behaviour, it may continue being amoral.

Heteronomy

This stage is characterised by the child's obedience to external authority, which could be from parents, elders, teachers and from religious authority. The child's behaviour is controlled by the adult through reward and punishment and it is disciplined by artificial consequences. The external control is a necessity in order to control the natural impulses of the child. The external controls may combine within themselves meaningful guidance and training by the adult. During such guided control, the child is like an apprentice under the adult. According to Norman J. Bull the stage of heteronomy is not an end by itself and should not be so. It can be a means to an end if it is properly utilised by the adult. It is no doubt an essential stage of moral development.

If exercised rationally, it turns out to be beneficial to the child while if otherwise it makes the child ever subservient to others in its moral capacity. Hence the adult should consider heteronomy as a stage fit for sowing the seeds of autonomy. In other words it should be like a discipline imposed from outside with the object of developing in the child self-discipline. This means that heteronomy must come to an end at some point of time during the period of child's moral development. It is strongest at the ages 7 to 9.

Parents, teachers and others in charge of training children in moral behaviour must remember that children need to be guided and advised for making them learn better morals rather than being threatened and punished. They must explain to the child the reasons for the particular type of behaviour expected of them and also the consequences that may probably follow if the behaviour were to be otherwise. The child should also be encouraged to accept and discharge such simple responsibilities which he can easily take rather than deny all responsibilities making him unfit for exercising any freedom of thinking and action.

Socionomy

While heteronomy is a stage full of external control this is a stage of external-internal control. During this stage the child's moral judgement is shaped by social forces. The child becomes conscious of himself and his self respect, feels responsible and likes to establish healthy relationship with others in the society. The members of the society in turn, exercise control over the child through their remarks of praise or blame, approval or disapproval of his actions. These evoke in the child certain feelings such as of confidence or fear of social boycott and attitudes such as obedience and cooperation. In this process the individual gets socialised and develops morally also.

Autonomy

This is a stage of purely internal moral development, a period of self-rule for the individual who imposes moral codes on himself by himself. He feels that it is in the best interest to himself and to the society of which he is a member and so it is his duty to lead a morally pure life. His action are guided by his conscience and the nature of discipline is self-discipline. It is a stage when the individual is capable of taking moral decisions on his own without any fear or fervour. Further whatever was there in him as sense of shame during the stage of socionomy is now replaced by a sense of guilt. This presupposes in him an ability to see himself through the eyes of others. His moral consciousness or conscience is aroused. According to Norman J. Bull conscience is born out of emotions, critical reasoning and the application of one's own moral principles to particular situations. As has already been said conscience develops in every individual by stages from childhood onwards. As the child grows in human society the external controls are gradually replaced by the corresponding internal controls. These may even be called abilities acquired by the individual.

Piaget's pioneering research on moral development in children helped him to recognise only two stages, namely, heteronomy and autonomy. While Kohlberg went further and identified six major stages of moral development, each of which reveals a different kind of motivation for acting morally or for forming moral judgement. Norman Bull on the other hand, has recognised four stages of moral development, and these are in the chronological order of age development of the child.

1.5. FACTORS AFFECTING MORAL JUDGEMENT OF CHILDREN

Parental Behaviour

Psychologists, educators and sociologists all agree that family influence happens to be the most significant single influence during child development. In the words of Thomson (1969), "Home influences probably outweigh the effects of all other environmental impacts combined in determining the fundamental organisation of children's behaviour." The significance of home can also be inferred from the words of Miller (1973):

"Home is the child's world in which the personality is shaped and his character formed. What the individual becomes depends to a large extent on the type of home in which he is born, upon the various environmental influences that play upon him within the domestic world during his earliest and most impressionable years."

Why do home and family play such an important role in shaping child's development, personality and behaviour? A number of explanations can be given. First, home influence is brought to bear upon the child during his earliest years and remains, in most cases, practically constant. Before influences outside home have had any real opportunity to make their impact felt, family would have shaped and influenced his personality through a variety of stimuli and situations gradually adjusting him to his environment and preparing him for his subsequent relations with the world (Donson, 1974).

Secondly, it is now a well known fact that habits are formed among children during their infancy years. Therefore, whether desirable habits are retained (and undesirable ones discontinued) shall depend primarily upon the home upbringing. It is in the family that a child gets a model for imitation. Children's impulses to admire and initiate are very powerful in their early years. The incessant repetition of stimuli brought about by close and intimate contacts with the family circle play upon their natural tendencies driving them to action. Kogan (1958) has indicated that:

"... the significant motive for the identification process is the desire to possess desirable characteristics of the model. The child wishes to possess adult qualities such as power, competence, strength and receipt of affection. The integrity displayed in family relationships is also a model for the child in developing his own sense of integrity."

Thirdly, the training, provided in the home is practical rather than being theoretical. Concrete situations are constantly dealt with. These situations are much more effective in the training of the young child than are the inculcation of principles of mere teaching of abstract ideas.

Fourthly, home is also very important from the point of view of socialisation of the child. It provides the most conducive environment for the development of those virtues which humanise life and make society possible. Schmielder (1973) points out that family is perhaps the best institution for socialization:

"The experiences in the family tend to liberate and bring into play spiritual forces which would remain undeveloped in any other system of upbringing. The small but intimate circle of family guarding, as it does, such manifold and deep feelings, afford to human personality a development far richer and far more secure than the best conceivable institutions could possibly give."

According to the psychoanalytic theory also, social values and controls are largely interiorised (made an integral part of the child's super-ego) on the basis of early parent-child interactions (Elkind, 1966; Illich, 1971). The foundations of children's social attitudes and skills which, in turn, are determined by the patterns of dependence-independence, ascendance-submission, cooperation competition have their genesis in early parent child interactions. These go a long way in shaping a child's personality and adjustment.

The importance of home in these areas has been further described by Dinkmeyer (1965) as:

"It is the home in which the child first experiences the meaning of love. It is here that he comes to experience the give and take of family life. A child who cannot get along with his siblings may eventually have some difficulty in getting along with others. The family has a most significant role to play in the development of personality. The customs and beliefs of our society are first handed down within the family. Here the child first observes and then internalizes. The values of parents, social, political and religious beliefs and customs are transmitted via the family."

Home can provide a splendid opportunity to the child to imbibe many moral qualities. It all depends on the conduct and behaviour of the elder members of the family whose actions and attitudes are imitated by children. Honesty, sincerity, integrity, industry, courage and discipline on the part of parents will have chastening effect on the child regarding the development of the right kind of moral behaviour. If thoughts, words and actions of parents are immoral they exert adverse influence on the child. Therefore the parents behaviour and conduct should be worthy of emulation. The elderly members of the family should teach children how to behave morally and responsively by their own examples. Example is better than precept children must be trained in showing respect to their elders and teachers and to all things that are worthy and noble. Parents should refrain from using vulgar uncultured words in their conversation. As is the father so is the son. Parents should emphasise good work habits, value learning and good character, set high expectations for their children, stay informed about their children's progress and monitor their children's activities.

We must note therefore that a good deal will have been learnt unconsciously from parents – perhaps more than is learnt from their deliberate efforts at moral upbringing, since children are more likely to learn to do as their parents do than as their parents say, to pay more attention to what they practice than to what they preach. This means that they will have acquired, probably uncritically, most of the attitudes of their parents. The unthinking racial prejudice of some young children would seem certainly to derive from this source.

It also means that in those situations where their parents' practices and precepts are divergent, the children's moral attitudes are likely to be highly confused. This is a major source of those double standards of moral behaviour that are to be observed throughout society, the inconsistency of "one rule for myself and another for the rest of the world" was incompatible with the notion of a rational morality. Young people are likely to be highly confused by parents who steal quite unashamedly from their places of employment but punish their children for behaving in what appears to them to be the same way, by parents whose attitude to sexual matters generally is liberal but who try to insist on firm sexual discipline in their own children.

It is not only parents who are a source of moral learning of this kind. Siblings, other immediate family members and many other adults will play their part too. Other adults too, either by accident or design, will influence children and young people morally through any kind of contact they have with them, so-called "charismatic" personalities being particular influential. For the most part, attitudes will be caught from such sources rather than taught by them.

The peer group too is a particularly fruitful source of values, especially at adolescence, and will play a major part in determining the value positions young people adopt and the behaviour pattern they come to feel they ought to conform to a point. This source of learning will give rise again to conflicts of values which are particularly difficult for the young person to resolve without the sensitive help of the teacher or another adult. Nor should we assume that, because the peer group is particular influential at adolescence, it is not important at other ages and stages; at the "gang" stage of the seven and eight year old it is perhaps equally important. Piaget's claims that not only does moral learning derive from this sources but also operative activities of the development of autonomy. On the other hand, we should not forget, as Kohlberg points out, that isolates can be morally developed as other children.

Parental influence is usually very great in the case of young children, while the peer group comes into the ascendant at adolescence. All combine, however, in varying degrees of strength and influence to create the moral content of each child's value system upon which the moral educator must work. They present him with three major problems., For firstly, they are lead to a great variety of learning, attitudes, beliefs and values. Secondly, there is a similar variety in the manner in which pupils will have come to hold these beliefs. And thirdly, in all cases, much of the learning and many of these attitudes, beliefs and values are unconscious, or, at least, are held uncritically. For either they are the result of unconscious influence and absorption that will entail uncritical acceptance or, as in the case of an authoritarian approach, by say organised religion or parents of particularly strong and dogmatic convictions, they are the result of deliberate attempts to secure uncritical acceptance. Because of this they are often in conflict with each other and lead to double standards of behaviour of a kind that cannot be accepted as rational nor, therefore, as constituting a moral education. Thus, the unreflective and uncritical nature of this learning make the moral educator's task an especially difficult one, since he must help his pupils to become conscious of them before he can encourage them to reflect critically on them and to make a reasoned appraisal of them.

At present parents are failing in their duty in giving proper attention to the socialisation of their children. They must find time to see that their children are brought up in moral surroundings and they should inculcate moral values which control the mind in the right direction. It trains the mind to identify good from bad and to appreciate and accept what is legally permitted by the society thereby making for proper moral judgements.

Child Rearing Practices

Although the optimal conditions for healthy child development have not yet been identified, research has provided many important clues. No doubt the present generation has more adequate information than any previous one on how child develop and how various methods of child rearing influence this development. In recent years, psychologists, educators and parents have argued the case for permissiveness in child rearing as opposed to the old-fashioned discipline. But there is a general agreement today a child can be just as handicapped though in a different way by a lack of discipline, as by overly severe restraints. It has been seen that high but realistic parental standards and expectations help children develop such a frame of reference and in doing so foster self esteem and self-confidence whereas parents who want them to enjoy themselves tend to have children with low self-esteem (Coopersmith, 1967).

It is empirically and generally believed that children acquire their fundamental values and attitudes from their parents, especially due to the child rearing practices (Bales, 1955; Sears, 1957; Mead, 1955). The best nurture for a child is provided – (i) in home (ii) primarily with mother's affection, (iii) in an interact family consisting of an unseparated father and mother, (iv) providing continuity in the child's upbringing and (v) in an atmosphere of loving acceptance.

The development of a child is influenced by the child-rearing practices in the society. Child rearing means "socialisation" the process by with a child, born into a given society, becomes a social being. Robert R. Sears and others (1957) describe that child rearing practices refer generally to all the interactions between the parents and their children. The interactions include the parents' expression of attitudes, values, interests and beliefs as well as their care-taking and training behaviour. According to Jersild (1957), a child's personality is the product of an interplay between influences in the environment and forces of heredity. Smart and Smart (1966) held that the unfolding of an individual's potentialities is determined by the type of the environment he is surrounded with.

The first two years of life a-re the formative years when the foundation for child's future development is laid. The family influence is paramount during this period, as the interactions of the child in the first two to three years is entirely confined to the family members, and the child internalises whatever he perceives around him. The child considers his parents as models for his behaviour and his adjustment to life.

The child develops patterns of social behaviour similar to those of his parents. The goal of all child rearing is to develop in the child the capacity for adjustment as prescribed by the cultural system to which the child belongs. Throughout the centuries, there have been shifts in the culturally approved child-training methods. Certain contemporary problems, as breast-feeding and emotional care of children during illness were discussed as far back as the sixteenth and seventeenth centuries. Since the turn of this century the issues of child rearing has been much discussed with the result that there has been a marked shift from rigid discipline to an understanding of the child and his needs and the adults' obligations to meet his needs.

In the Indian setting, the family has a major role in the child's socialisation. However, it is not the only possible agent, as the process which, though begins in the home, does not end there. The outside world also makes significant impact on the child as he is exposed to a succession of persons, groups and institutions each of which imposes its own expectations, rewards and punishments on the child and contributes to shaping the development of his skills, values and pattern of behaviour through positive and negative reinforcements.

Child rearing includes much more than providing a child- food, shelter, and clothing which are the basic for growth. The growing child has to be provided opportunities for the realisation of his potentialities with love and affection. Numerous studies conducted independently (Ripple, Spitz, Bender and Bowlby (1953)) have proved the importance of love, and the undesirable effect of deprivation. It has been observed that lack of love can hamper the physical, mental and emotional growth of the child.

Child rearing practices differ from culture to culture, and also among different groups within the same culture. They are influenced, among other things, by the educational level, economic condition and traditional value system of the family and caste or subcaste group. Evidence shows that there are in fact social class differences in child-rearing practices that affect children's moral development. Studies by Sears *et al.* (1957), Kohn (1958), Kohlberg (1966), Kay (1968) and Bull (1969), to mention but a few, all suggest that children from families of higher social status show greater maturity in moral judgement than those from lower social class backgrounds. Religious and regional differences have also been found to exist in the child rearing patterns in India. Research by Haan, Smith and Block conclusively point out the influence of child rearing practices on the moral development of the child.

Emotional Maturity

Emotion and feelings are state of affective experiences and they serve distinct purposes for individuals in adjustments and determination of their behaviour. In fact, nearly every behaviour is atleast partly determined by the affective state of the individual at that point of time. Since the beginning, psychologists have been attempting to bring out the difference between feelings and emotions. Even now difference of opinion about whether they are of the same affective state or are different from each other only in their degree of intensity exists. Some consider feelings to be mild and "exist as background states" whereas emotions are intense, stirred up experiences involving a greater part of the central nervous system, endocrine and visceral systems of the physiology. According to psychologists, aesthetic feelings, sex, annoyances or irritation and affection are feelings, whereas anger, fear, jealousy and love are regarded as emotions.

A variety of opinion, some theoretical and others based on controlled experiments, exists regarding the earlier manifestation of emotional experiences. Those psychologists who believe in the maturational basis of emotional development stress that the infant is capable of emotional experiences at the time of birth, if not earlier. Freud, the famous theorist, wrote that even the foetus could have feelings though he recognised that the human infant "comes into the world more unfinished."

The most famous of all experiments on emotional responses of infants, is the classical experiment conducted by Watson when he presented various kinds of stimuli to neonates and recorded their reactions. He concluded that the new-borns exhibited three kinds of unlearnt emotional responses, i.e., fear, rage and love. He postulated that the three fundamental and primary emotions are the basis on which varieties of emotional expressions in older children and adults are an out-growth. Further researches have not borne out Watson's contentions, but his work highlighted two important aspects, namely, his rigorous experimental approach to the study of emotions and his rejection of the 'heredity theory' of emotion. He says all varieties of emotional experiences present in the adult are there in the child and are totally inherited.

Hurlock (1955) has pointed out a few characteristics which distinguish the emotional response of children from that of adults. In the case of children the intensity of reaction to a relatively mild and critical situation is the same in the case of either "positive" or "negative" emotions, that is, irrespective of the magnitude of the stimuli the emotional outburst in children is always high. The emotional reaction of children is not in proportion to the intensity of the situation and from an adult's point of view they "overract" to any stimuli however mild it may be. With learning and acquiring of social values there comes the understanding of emotional reactions that are not appropriate and the child learns to exercise control over the expression of emotions.

Secondly, a child's emotions are brief transitory and short-lived. It is there -as long as the pleasant or the unpleasant situation is affecting him, and may be for sometime more in both cases. But in adults and older children the emotional feelings are of a longer duration and affect their behaviour much after the situation is not present.

Thirdly, the frequency of emotional response is more in the case of children than in the case of adults. With age and further social development and learning the child learns through experience, the societal impact and tries to restrain frequent emotional experiences. Again, children of the same age react in various and myriad ways to similar or the same situation, that is, their reactions are flexible. Advance in age, delimits the scope of emotional responses and becomes appropriate to the situation giving rise to it. Also with advancing age and social conformity some emotions become weaker and some stronger.

Both maturation and learning determine the development of nearly all aspects of human behaviour. The growth and development of sensory processes, muscular activities, and also that of intellectual functions and affective states are influenced by 'maturation' as well as 'learning'. The most important factor is motivation. Because of their inter-related roles, it becomes extremely difficult in many situations, to study the influence of one to the exclusion of the other. Yet, attempts have been made to evaluate the role of each separately in understanding human development.

Emotions are a result of social learning, given the needed maturational basis. When the stimuli acquire meanings for the child and is perceived as a threat or pleasantness the child emotionally reacts to it accordingly. Obviously in the process of growth, the child comes cross may objects, which directly does not cause him discomfort or concern to arouse emotions. In the process of learning of social values some objects acquire meanings and the child relates to some of these day to day objects and perceives them as situations to which he should react emotionally.

As a result of social learning, the child learns to modify, delimit the intensity, the scope and the frequency of emotional expressions, to conform to the socio-cultural values in which he grows up, that is, from the gross reactions manifest in early childhood, the child comes to learn more 'refined' ways of emotional expressions. Sometimes, this restriction of frequency and intensity of emotional expression is carried too far to lead to repression of emotion which becomes pent up inside and need expressive release. If this release is consistently denied it can lead to serious disturbances in personality and mental health. Moreover, the emotions felt by the child become more complex with further development and social learning, depending on the social, economic and cultural milieu he grows up in, as the 'exposure' to social values and education are very different from one society to the other, differing from one social stratum to another.

If the child fails to conform to the social norms and values in his expression of emotions it leads to maladjustments which could make him a misfit in that society. Children growing with emotional problems which, when unresolved, further render them maladjusted in the adult years. The parental influences on the emotional development of children is an extremely important factor. Issues like the socio-economic status of the parents, education and other such variables like child rearing practices, relationship between parents themselves and with the child, are the major determining factors of normal emotional development of the child. Juvenile delinquency, criminality, lack of drive, heightened frustrations and anxieties, withdrawals from reality, etc. are some of the effects of emotional disturbances and experiences of early childhood due to faulty parent-child relationships and other variables as mentioned, which leave such tell-a-tale marks on the adult personality, rendering them maladjusted society, as has been amply highlighted by researches done in the West. In India, there is an extreme paucity of research directly related to emotional development and emotional maturity.

Some researches with a base on social development can be cited indirectly, as considerable extent depends upon normal emotional development of children. They are as follows: Murlidharan (1969) found that children from large size families i.e., family units consisting of three children showed significantly less of problem behaviour than the children from the families who have one or two children. The sample consisted of subjects in the age group of three to eight years and some of behaviour problems studied were, delinquency, unsocial behaviour, aggressiveness, etc. which are also related to abnormal emotional development. Kakkar's study (1970) attempted to explore the role of "family conflict" in the development of the child. Using a questionnaire he measured the extent of interparental conflict related to child-rearing problems and scholastic achievement.

Faizunisa and Parameshwaran (1965 & 1968) found a relationship between maternal behaviour and behaviour problems of children, possibly due to emotional disturbances. Prasad and Prasad (1975) on their study on pre-school children of working mothers found sex differences in the behaviour. They compared the behaviour of pre-school children of employed mothers with non-school going children of non-employed mothers in specifically created play situations. The authors concluded that pre-school education did not seem to affect adversely the personality of the child in terms of anxiety and nervousness, etc. While examining the effects of mother's working status on children it was found that whereas male children in the working group was socially more participative and emotionally mature than the male children of non-working group, they tended to have higher scores on nervous habits and the girls more anxious.

There are many such studies conducted but the size of sample selected to such studies locally and purposively do not lend children to generalisations. In conclusion, it can be said that emotional development of children is one of the most complicated processes and it depends as much upon the physiological maturation of the endocrine system, the neutral system, the visceral system and the autonomic nervous system as on the learning and environmental factors. This aspects of development is one of the most important in the sense that its normal development would lead to well adjusted personalities, whereas abnormalities in its development could have far reaching consequences from maladjustments to acute psycho-social pathology.

A wide variety of factors in the environment in which a child grows, influences his growth of emotions and their expressions. Parental influence which is maximum in childhood is the most crucial of all factors which helps normal emotional development. In fact the major causes of later emotional maladjustments can be traced back to a unhappy childhood, broken home, parental conflicts and such other factors.

Anxieties, phobias, depression, nervousness, insecurity, aggressiveness are but a few of the problems which are an outcome of such situations which leave tell-a-tale marks on the adult personality. Also as the child emotionally develops with the process of conditioning and de-conditioning in his natural environment, wrong associations of stimuli with emotions could lead to emotional disturbances and affected adulthood.

Thus, leaving aside factors of heredity and maturational growth the environmental factors could be controlled and manipulated to offer conducive surroundings for the optimum emotional development, maturity and adjustment of the child. The provision to the child of a happy home, optional exposure and a good learning environment in school and society for social learning would lead to normal emotional development and maturity.

Personality Traits

Personality is like a completed jig-saw puzzle. It comprises of physical, mental, emotional, moral, social aspects, habits, character, intelligence and sentiments to become the integrated whole. It is a process which goes on in a sequential order. Thus personality is what a man really is. According to J.B. Watson, personality is the result of what we start with and what we have lived through. It is the 'reaction mass' as a whole. According to Allport it is the dynamic organisation within the individual of those psychological systems that determine his unique adjustment to his environment.

Allport (1962) has pointed out that there are approximately 18,000 terms in English language designating distinctive and personal forms of behaviours and these are called personality traits. In the present study, by personality traits one would mean, those distinguishing characteristics which define an individual in relation to his adjustment to the environment.

Jung (1959) spoke of the total personality as the psyche which he held consists of a number of separate interaction systems. These include the ego, the personal unconscious, the collective unconscious, its archetypes, the personal, the anima or animus and the shadow. In addition to these interacting systems Jung held that in the attitudes of introversion and extroversion the function of thinking, feeling, sensing and institution as well as the self comprise the psyche.

Jung (1923) held that we can distinguish two typical behaviour patterns which arise out of the attitude of people the extrovert "type" as he described, is outgoing and concerned with the external, objective world. In Freudian terminology extroversion was an outward turning of the libido. For Long however, it meant that extrovertedness is thinking, feeling senses and acting in a direct manner. The extrovert is out going whether it be the intellectual activities, in physical activities, or in feelings. If the state of extroversion becomes habitual with an individual he is an extroverted type. Introversion on the other hand, means a turning inward toward one's self. A negative relation is implied, even expressed. Interest recede towards the self. When introversion is habitual, the individual is described as an introvert type. Both attitude are present in everyone, but one dominates and the other is subordinated.

The introversion-extroversion concept has had more influence on psychology than any other in Jung's idea about personality. It emphasizes the polarity principle which is probably one of the most universal idea we find among personality theorists. We see this principle in operation also in Jung's notion of the personal unconscious and the collective unconscious in his anima and animus concept and in other dimensions of his personality theory.

Eysenck's Research Findings

In his first major research effort (Eysenck, 1947) studying a group of ten thousand soldier subjects was able to isolate two variables. The first was bi-polar dimension of introversion-extroversion which Jung had already identified clinically. Eysenck's findings then confirmed Jung's theory. Another dimension which Eysenck later identified was neuroticism.

Neurotic introverts show a tendency to develop anxiety and depression symptoms that are characterised by observational tendencies, such as irritability and apathy. According to their own statement, their feelings are easily hurt, they are self-conscious, nervous, given to feeling of inferiority, mood day-dream easily, keep in the background of social occasions and suffer from sleeplessness. Salivary secretion is inhabited. Their intelligence is comparatively high. Their vocabulary is excellent and they tend to be persistent. They are generally accurate but slow, they excel at finishing work. Their level of aspiration is unduly high. But they tend to under rate their own performance with that their aesthetic preferences are towards the quiet old fashioned type of picture. In aesthetic creation, they produce compact designs, often having a concrete subject. They do not appreciate jokes very much and sex jokes in particular are not much favoured. Their handwriting is distinctive.

In comparison neurotic extrovert show a tendency to develop hysterical conversion symptoms and a hysterical attitude to their symptoms. Furthermore, they show little energy, narrow interests, have a bad work history and are hypochondrical. According to their own statement they are troubled by stammer or stutter, are accident prone frequently off work through illness, disgruntled and trouble by aches and pains. In their body build, horizontal growth predominates over vertical growth. Their intelligence is comparatively low, their vocabulary poor and they show extreme lack of persistence. They tend to be quick but inaccurate; they are bad at finishing work their level of aspiration is low, but they tend to over-rate their own performance. They are not very rigid and show great intrapersonal variability. Their aesthetic preference are towards the colourful, modern type of picture. In aesthetic creation, they produce scattered designs, often having abstract subjects. They appreciate jokes and are particularly fond of sex jokes. Their handwriting is distinctive.

Eysenck (1953) felt that Jung's introversion-extroversion typology and Kretschmers schizothymia cyclothymia typology were not identical. He set out to test the hypothesis that there was a difference from Jung's introversion-extroversion dimension. In his research, Eysenck (1953) found and described three primary dimensions of personality.

1) Introversion versus extroversion,
2) Normality (stability) versus neurotism (Instability) and
3) Psychoticism.

The first two basic dimensions above account for a good part of individual personality:

1) Introversion versus extroversion, and
2) Normality (stability) versus neurotism (Instability)

Eysenck (1953) has been an avid researcher. He has stimulated many others to study the phenomena in which he has taken an interest. Some of the reported finding support his theories. While others contradict them Eysenck has tried to explain personality as genetically caused. His major efforts have been to develop and test the cause of personality types. He traces nuerotism to the automatic nervous system and introversion-extroversion to the central nervous system.

If any agreement exists as to the structure of temperament it is in the first two dimensions with which Eysenck has been concerned. Introversion-extroversion and neurotism also referred to as anxiety. Raymond Cattle (1965) and Guilford (1959), Gough (1957), Block (1967), Taylor (1953) and others find support for these same personality dimensions in their research. We may conclude then, that the dimension of temperament have been extensively explored that such dimensions exist. It is of interest to note that researches in related areas have also been concerned with these same dimensions of personality.

Meaning of Introversion – Extroversion - Ambiversion

Introversion and extroversion are the source of individual difference. One interpretation is that introversion-extroversion is not a single dimension of personality but a term that refers to a complex set of characteristics. Another interpretation is that it is a basic trait of personality.

Introversion and extroversion are the terms used to describe the direction our life force takes. According to Freud, introversion and extroversion are merely two phases of libido activity. He emphasised that when the projection of libido outside the ego is thwarted, then there is a tendency for the libido to become introjected that is to turn back to the stages of earlier libido-freedom.

An introverted type demonstrate hesitating defensive and reflicient behaviour, while the extrovert has an open and rally disposition, is easy in any situation forms attachment quickly and ventures confidentially into unknown situation in introvert the libido (life force) is directed towards the self rather than outside world; in the extrovert the libido is turned outward. The extrovert is not one who always and at all times behaves as an extrovert, nor is the introvert one who always and at all times remain a introvert. A person who is an introvert in certain society or during particular situation may become an extrovert in others.

Recent attempts at the measurement of the personality characteristics that introversion or extroversion is not merely an absence of the one and a development of the other. There are none but extremely abnormal cases that can be described as pure introverts or extroverts. The large majority are ambiverts, and exhibit both types of responses under varying situations. Therefore the intermediate version of introversion-extroversion is called ambiversion.

In the present study personality traits has been included as an independent variable and its relationship with moral judgement of adolescent children has been studied.

Socio-Economic Status

Evidence shows that there are in fact social class differences that affect children's moral development. Studies by Sears (1957), Kohn (1958), Kohlberg (1966), Kay (1968) and Bull (1969), to mention but a few, all suggest that children from families of higher social status show greater maturity in Moral Judgement than those from lower social class backgrounds.

Sex Differences

Studies by Soni (1984) and Bush (1981) have concluded that girls were better than boys in Moral Judgement and that adolescent girls have greater sensitivity to moral dilemma than boys.

Type of Management

Among the various environmental factors in human learning, the school is a very important one. The school has the unique and major responsibility of teaching certain skills and abilities while serving as the best medium for the most important types of learning. Schooling involves the interaction between the teacher and the pupils in the teaching-learning process. The set up of a school as a whole has a great influence on the development of attitudes and values.

1.6. NEED FOR THE STUDY

There is an awareness of the development of the world which is paradoxical in nature. While the aura of science and technology has reached the moon and almost reaching towards to Neptune, while a distance of million miles are now synchronised into hours and minutes, while any happening in any corner of the world could be seen on the television, a distance between two souls, between the world of emotions of two nations, society, religion and caste and community have increased considerably. This however gives an impression of equivocal development in general.

The atmosphere of conflict and turmoil has increased. The rate of crime and delinquency has increased. Socio-psychological health of the people has declined. There is almost a decay of most comprehensive human values that used to maintain integrity of society and humanity in genera. The core human values which sustain and foster peaceful co-existence are being eroded by the process of modernisation and technological development. Therefore the flow of modernisation has to have some comprehensive values corresponding to the general quality of life in order to maintain equilibrium in the society.

It is quite often seen that frustration among parents is also increasing with the face of development. It is obvious that accumulated frustration would definitely reflect on the growing child. How and to what extent children could be saved from the "conflicting model" of parenting should also be considered as an integrated package of education of moral and social values.

Education in reality is also posing a serious threat to the processes of moral development. The teachers in general are trying to shift the school responsibility of the children to the family responsibility. This new phenomena which is no more confined to a single area of the country, which is now even openly criticized, is encouraging children during early steps to develop dependency to a greater extent. Phenomena of mass copying, getting home work done by others at younger age, would be a bad facilitator in developing moral and social values. Because children learn what exists in society, their thinking, liking, perception, planning all these are largely influenced by the ingredients of socio-cultural realities in which they grow.

There is a need to analyse the loss of important and essential values, may be traditional and old, but which are highly cherished values. Whether the concern for brotherhood, neighbourhood and parenthood is diminishing and all these are sacrificed in the process of achieving the material world? One of the psychological consequences of modernisation is that it is perhaps, making a man more mechanical in thinking, attitude, action and interaction which would directly hamper the growing world of children. Under such circumstances, what kind of preventive approach as to be adopted and how the children from the early stage could be kept away from the growing world of bewilderment and in what way the package of moral and social values relating to the survival, integration, promotion of human values could be made possible are the major issues. These issues are specifically in the context of school children which by and large is known as period of foundation.

The foundation stones for such a superstructure cannot be laid in quick sand or in loose soil which cannot hold the foundation. What is needed for a life of ever lasting happiness is the integrity and a basis of a deep committed morality, which itself is founded on universal and all embracing principles of human co-existence and co-operation and laws of harmony and peace.

Today the whole world is suffering from the lethal disease of moral anaemia. Most people adopt illegal and immoral means to grind their own axe. They do not hesitate to harm others in achieving their selfish ends. Today a man sacrifices every ideal and joins the mad rat race of materialism. This moral anaemia is working like a strong negative catalyst by causing a dangerous delay in individual and national progress and development. The moral degradation of youth is causing serious concern to parents, teachers and community members. The erosion of values and increasing cynicism in our modern society particularly younger generation, has brought to forces the need for readjustments in the curriculum in order to make education a forceful tool for cultivation of social, ethical and moral values (National policy on education – 1986 – National curriculum) which would ultimately lead to ethical decision making and acceptable moral judgements. In the light of the above discussion the investigator felt an imperative need to undertake the present study.

1.7. STATEMENT OF THE PROBLEM

A Study of Moral Judgement of students in relation to their Parental Behaviour, Child Rearing Practices, Emotional Maturity and Personality Traits.

1.8. SCOPE OF THE PROBLEM

It was intended through the present investigation to study the Moral Judgement of students in relation to sociological, psychological and other variables. The independent variables were Parental Behaviour, Child Rearing Practices, Emotional Maturity, Personality Traits, Socio-Economic Status, Sex and Type of School Management under which the students were pursuing their studies. Moral Judgement was considered as the dependent variable. It comprised all the five dimensions of moral judgement namely – Honesty, Truthfulness, Non-violence, Obedience and Justice.

Parental behaviour was measured by using the modified and adapted version of Children's Report of Parental Behaviour Inventory originally developed by Dr. Uma Saxena and Dr. N.K. Saxena and later adapted by the investigator for this study. Child Rearing Practices Test by Pal and Karim, Emotional Maturity Scale by Dr. Tara Sabapathy, Personality Traits (Introversion and Extroversion) Inventory by Kundu and Kuppuswamy's Socio-Economic Status Scale was used to measure the independent variables respectively.

The tools were administered on a sample of 500 students studying in the secondary schools of Bangalore City. The composition of the sample was that there were 250 boys and 250 girls studying in three different types of management, namely, private aided, private unaided and government schools. The design followed in the process and sample selection procedure is given in the third chapter.

The data were collected by the researcher herself by personally visiting the schools. All precautions were observed to restore normal condition while collecting data. The data were analysed to test the hypotheses as stated. Mainly the purpose of the study were to examine the independent variables that were significantly related to Moral Judgement and to find out whether the independent variables namely – Parental Behaviour, Child Rearing Practices, Emotional Maturity, Personality Traits, Socio-Economic Status, Sex and Type of Management accounted for significant differences in the dependent variable Moral Judgement. It was also the intention of the investigator to examine the nature of interaction that existed between the independent variables and the dependent variable.

Considering all these, the present study of Moral Judgement of students in relation to their Parental Behaviour, Child Rearing Practices, Emotional Maturity, Personality Traits, Socio-Economic Status, Sex and Type of Management was undertaken with the objectives.

1.9. OBJECTIVES OF THE STUDY

1. To find out the relationship between Moral Judgement of students and their Parental Behaviour.
2. To find out the relationship between Moral Judgement of students and Child Rearing Practices.
3. To find out the relationship between Moral Judgement of students and their Emotional Maturity.
4. To find out the relationship between Moral Judgement of students and their Personality Traits.

5. To find out the differences if any in Moral Judgement of students as per differences in their Parental Behaviour.
6. To find out the differences if any in Moral Judgement of students as per differences in the Child Rearing Practices (father form and mother form).
7. To find out the differences if any in Moral Judgement of students as per differences in their Emotional Maturity.
8. To find out the differences if any in Moral Judgement of students as per differences in their Personality Traits (Introversion-Extroversion-Ambiversion).
9. To find out the differences if any in Moral Judgement of students as per differences in their Parental Socio-economic status.
10. To find out the differences if any in Moral Judgement of students as per differences in sex.
11. To find out the differences if any in Moral Judgement of students as per differences in Type of Management.
12. To find out the main and interaction effect on the levels of moral judgement of students when the possible pairs of independent variables and their levels in this regard are considered.
13. To give educational implications in the light of the conclusions and also to make recommendations for further research.

1.10. LIMITATIONS OF THE STUDY

1. The study is limited to students in the City of Bangalore. There were as many as 842 secondary schools in the City of Bangalore at the time of data collection, out of which only 20 schools have been selected. Though Bangalore is an urban area, of late the growth of Bangalore City is phenomenal because many people are migrating from rural areas as well are added to the

population of Bangalore. Thus, the limitation that the study is confined to an urban area may not be limitation in the true sense when considered from this point of view.

2. The investigator has selected only students as sample for the research study. This has been done due to the implicit limitations that have been there in the study from the point of view of cost and effort.
3. The researcher could include only a few independent variables in the present study. This has been purposefully done to do an indepth analysis of these variables.

1.11. AN OVERVIEW OF THE STUDY

In this chapter a brief explanation of the problem, need for the study, objectives of the study is discussed along with the scope and limitations of the study. In the second chapter the review of related literature has been presented with its relevance and significance for the present study. Chapter III deals with research design or methodology of the problem under study. In this connection it also gives a brief description of the variables, hypotheses, sampling procedure and the tools used for collecting and analysing the data. In the fourth chapter the obtained data is subjected to statistical analysis. Discussion of the results and interpretation of the data are also presented. Finally the last chapter gives the summary of the complete study. Important findings of the study are highlighted and recommendations made on the basis of these findings are given. Finally the educational implications have been presented.

CHAPTER II

REVIEW OF RELATED LITERATURE

The present chapter deals with the review of related literature and studies on moral judgement and related correlates. To carry out the review for the purposes of the present study the following two key concepts have been extracted from the research problem and the review is organised around them (i) Trends of research on moral development and moral judgement and (ii) relationship between the dependent variable moral judgement and the independent variables, namely- parental behaviour, child rearing practices, emotional maturity, personality traits, socio-economic status, sex differences and type of management. The trends studies on moral development and moral judgement are tackled in a general way to examine the extent of coverage of research done in this area in the past few decades in India as well as abroad. It is also the intention of the investigator to project the research gap that has been existing in this area and to focus on areas that have received priority and attention in this regard. In such a pursuit the relationship of moral judgement with the possible variables with which it has been explored for the relation have been considered.

When the relationship between the dependent variable moral judgement with the independent variables have been considered it has been to a large extent done in a very specific way. Finally an attempt has been made to bring together the results of the existing research to highlight the relationship among studies and to identify where gaps and weaknesses exist.

2.1. TREND STUDIES ON MORAL DEVELOPMENT AND MORAL JUDGEMENT

Moral development cannot be studied in isolation from other aspects of development, e.g., physical, intellectual, emotional and social. There are various studies to show the effect of these developments upon moral development. It is difficult for a child to develop mature moral understanding, strong moral sentiment or prompt moral action if he is intellectually deficient, emotionally affectless, socially isolated or physically handicapped. The relationship, however, is a complicated one. For example, a certain amount of intellectual maturity is necessary for moral understanding and moral judgement; but that does not imply that the more intelligent a person is he is not necessarily a more moral person. Again, the emotionally affectless becomes a psychopath; but excessive emotions may also lead to immoral behaviour. That is why we find wide differences among the research findings in this area.

Moral development has been studied under three perspectives – social learning theory, psychoanalytical theory and cognitive development theory. The social learning theory accepts moral learning as a socially learned behaviour transmitted by direct teaching or imitation. The psychoanalytical theory emphasises the internalisation of standards and values. The cognitive developmental approach represented by Piaget (1930) and Kohlberg (1964) focuses on the kind of reasoning or moral judgement that people use in making decisions or in understanding justice.

Kohlberg's work has been followed by a large number of empirical researches to confirm his findings that people from a wide sample of cultures follow the same stages of moral development. Researches also confirm that few people reach the post-conventional stage of moral development. However, some of the findings speak in a somewhat different voice. Turiel (1978) feels that Kohlberg's stage system fails to deal with much of the child's knowledge about justice. Nucci (1981) feels that a distinction should be made between morality and social convention.

Research studies on moral development have identified that child rearing practices can affect moral development to a large extent. Parents' consistency of behaviour and reasoned dialogue with the child (Kohlberg), warm and nurturant parents (Hoffman, 1981), use of punishment as a preferred method of discipline (Hoffman and Saltztein) physical punishment (Burton), are some of such positive and negative factors.

Peer reasoning has been found to be an important factor in moral development. Social participation (Keasby, 1971; Kohlberg, 1981) awareness of the other person's perspectives (Hughes, Tingle and Samin, 1981), and heterogeneity of students' moral reasoning in an individual (Berkowitz, 1981) are some such factors of moral development.

Regarding the areas of research documented in the Fifth Survey of Research on moral development, moral judgement and values, the investigator identified four studies on values and value education, eleven studies on value development and value orientation, seven studies on moral judgement, three studies on value clarification, one study on value patterns, one study on values preferences, two on instructional strategies, one on measurement of values, one on stage structure of value development, one on concept and implementation, and three on content analysis.

After analysing the objectives, methodology, research tools and findings of the research abstracts, the investigator found that although researches have been done in some important areas of moral development and moral education, many more areas remain untouched. Not more than 10% of the universities in India are interested in conducting research work on moral education. It may be due to the fact that it is difficult to get data for such researches as very few institutions have provision for moral education. In spite of the concrete suggestions given by the Sri Prakash Committee for moral education in schools and colleges, the recommendations made by the Kothari Commission on the issue and the recent emphasis on value-oriented education, very little provision has been made in our schools and colleges for such education. If there is no education, how can there be research on education? Again, there are more researches in the area of moral development than in the area of moral education. Most researches that are being done are more psychological than educational. A few researches are on correlates of moral development. Existing value patterns have been surveyed but researches on inculcation of values through educational intervention are very few in number. It is necessary that while doing research work, more stress should be given to formulation of educational objectives, preparation of instructional materials–both curricular and co-curricular–development of strategies and trying out those materials through experimental-design of researches. From the analysis of the abstracts, the investigator found that experimental researches are very few in number. The majority of the researches have been done in the area of value judgement and some on moral judgement, which is a necessary step towards moral maturity. But it should be kept in mind that correct moral judgement is not the total issue. Education should be such that moral sentiments are awakened and moral conduct is produced. We know that there is often discrepancy and gap between moral judgement and moral behaviour. Researches should be done to develop such strategies that can minimise the gap. Researches should suggest how teachers, parents and the whole society can play their roles in inculcating moral values and moral behaviour in children and thus transform the society into a better society.

2.2. RELATIONSHIP BETWEEN DEPENDENT VARIABLE MORAL JUDGEMENT AND THE INDEPENDENT VARIABLES OF THE STUDY

As has been pointed out in the beginning of this chapter, in this section the review of related literature and studies have been presented under the headings given below.

1. Studies on Parental Behaviour and Moral Judgement
2. Studies on Child Rearing Practices and Moral Judgement
3. Studies on Emotional Maturity and Moral Judgement
4. Studies on Personality Traits and Moral Judgement
5. Studies on Socio-Economic Status and Moral Judgement
6. Studies on Sex Differences and Moral Judgement
7. Studies on Type of School Management and Moral Judgement

STUDIES ON PARENTAL BEHAVIOUR AND MORAL JUDGEMENT

Garg (1983), studied children's perception of parental disciplinary practice and its relation to development of personality needs, moral judgement and problem-solving ability. The sample consisted of 270 students selected by random sampling technique. Moral judgement was assessed with the help of Moral Judgement Test developed by Durganand Sinha and Meera Verma. The Personality Need Test developed by C.P. Sharma was also used. Analysis was done by ANOVA, Factorial Designs and Correlation Techniques. The important findings were moderate parental disciplinary practice significantly promoted a need for the development of moral judgement, need for achievement and need for change. It also indicated that the development of personality and moral judgement were closely related to the type of parental disciplinary practice.

Bhargava (1986) conducted a study on the development of moral judgement among children at concrete and formal operational stages and its relationship with home and educational environment. The sample consisted of students, parents and teachers. The tools used were The Sinha and Verma Moral Judgement Test (1968), The Sherry and Verma Family Relationship Inventory (1968), The Test of Moral Dilemma and an interview schedule for parents. Data was analysed using t test, Product Moment Co-efficient of Correlation, Factor Analysis and Regression. The findings of the study were, a significant development of moral judgement from one age group to the next successive age group. Home variables were significant predictors of moral judgement in terms of mother acceptance, socio-economic status and moral attitudes.

Rao (1984) conducted a study on moral judgement in children. The main objectives of the study were (1) to develop an instrument for moral judgement based on Kohlberg's theoretical constructs, (2) to develop an instrument to measure religious practices and moral judgement. A moral judgement questionnaire was constructed based on the theoretical constructs of Kohlberg's stage topology. The sample included 200 boys and 200 girls drawn from different classes. The major findings were that there was significant difference between age and moral reasoning at different stages and there was a significant relationship between levels of family religious practices and moral judgement scores, the latter being higher in the case of subjects coming from less rigid religious practices.

Parikh (1968) conducted a study on development of moral judgement and its relation to family environmental factor in India and American families. To assess the level of development the tools used were The Global Stage Scale and the Moral Maturity Scale. There were some significant difference in the findings of the American studies and the present day Indian families. In American studies the relationship of the family environmental factor to children's development of moral judgement is significantly positive where age does not count. In India age is important in determining the hierarchical interaction pattern in the family.

Johnson and Medinnus (1964) after careful review of the literature concluded that a good time is said to be one in which the child is given the fullest opportunity for self expression within the limits of parental acceptance and supervision. Such children display more realistic thinking, more mature judgement and more self-reliance.

Rani M. (1968) conducted a survey of moral development among children. The objectives of the investigation were (1) to study the pattern of morality among children, and (2) to analyse the developmental trends and influences operating on the process. The sample consisted of 350 children ranging from 6 to 11 years. Coloured Progressive Matrices, Moral Insight Test and Personal data form developed by the investigator were used for collecting the data. The findings were (1) knowledge of different moral values seemed to increase with an increase in age, (2) Respect was the most frequent moral value practiced by most children in their every day behaviour, closely associated with it were forgiveness and *punya*. Betrayal of faith, greed, anger and falsehood were some of the negative values which were quite frequent in their behaviour, (3) Parents influence in the acquisition and development of moral values in children was of vital significance.

Kapur (1986) studied the moral education of primary school children in sociological perspective. The methodology that was adopted was descriptive. The data was collected with the help of observation, schedule and Piagetian interviews on the acquisition of moral judgement by children. The data were analysed and interpreted in normative social interaction settings. The findings of the study were – the learning of religious belief and practice consisted of adult demonstration of the correct observance of certain events.

Hindu religious values were a part of children's socialisation in their homes and villages.

Walker and Taylor (1972) conducted a study on the family interactions and the development of moral reasoning. The sample was on 80 families with a total number of 240 individuals (Mother, Father and Child). The children were drawn from 4 different grades. In order to provide a range of developmental levels, ANOVA and ANCOVA were used. The important findings of the study were – (1) Parents play an influential role in their children's moral development. (2) 17 out of 80 children were unwilling to reveal their real life dilemma in the family session on patterns of moral reasoning. Correlational analysis of levels of moral reasoning revealed consistently positive but weak and non-significant relations between parents and children.

Gupta (1981) aimed at developing a parental preference inventory related to educational, emotional, social, moral, physical and vocational preferences for analysing the relationship of parental preferences with adolescents adjustment, personality, achievement and children's education at home and school. Through purposive sampling, 3,404 cases were involved at one stage or other of the study. Patterns of parental preferences were identified by the Parental Preference Inventory (PPI) prepared by the investigator along with Singh's Adolescent Personality Inventory and Saxena's Adjustment Inventory. The important findings of the study were: (1) parents as a group tended to show varying parental preferences in different spheres while some tended to exist as core preferences; those preferences were primarily focussed on higher academic achievement followed by the physical and social fields and tended to neglect influences of tradition, culture and Indian social norms.

In an early investigation, Ayer and Bernreuto (1937) found some interesting relationships between child's behaviour (as measured by Merril and Palmer Personality Rating

Scale) and parental practices and child discipline. They found that physical punishment tends to orient the child away from reality and makes him more dependent upon adult affection and attention. When children are permitted to profit from their own mistakes with a minimum of adult affection, interference, punishment and attention respectively, they tend to have better personalities.

Brown, Morrison and Couch (1950) found that traits like honesty, friendliness and responsibility tended to come from restrictive and autocratic homes. Mothers of prejudiced children demanded unquestioned obedience from the children. There seemed to be little opportunity for the child to try his own wings.

Watson (1957) concluded from his study that greater freedom provided by parents tended to be associated with more child initiative, less hostility and higher levels of spontaneity and originality respectively.

Davitz (1958) found that punishment and rejection give rise to fear; fear promotes defence reactions and defence reactions elicit further punishment. Thus a vicious circle is set up.

According to Hallowitz and Stulberg (1959), a child's feeling of rejection generates a vicious circle in the parent-child relationship. The child becomes anxious and insecure about whether or not his parents love him. He then tests them, retaliates, rebels or withdraws. The parents, in turn, feel unappreciated and rejected and their negative, hostile and rejecting feelings are further stirred up, aggravated and intensified.

In recent years, Sinha and Sadana (1973) have found that rejective behaviour on the part of parents increased the number of fears in children. This study also shows that children who are punished by their parents have more fear tendencies as compared to their counterparts. The rewarding behaviour of the parents was found to be less fear-provoking.

Ganagey (1973) reported the results of an unpublished study by Thurstone, Feldhusen and Benning. It was found that children who expressed deviant behaviour belonged to those families where the parental behaviour towards children was deviant.

Robinson (1975) conducted a comprehensive study on adolescents and reported that misconduct in schools is influenced by student boredom which in turn, is correlated with values, interest and the behaviour of parents.

Singh (1977) while studying dependence-proneness with perceived parental behaviour found that parents' loving attitude towards children leads to independence. On the other hand, parental rejection, protection and neglect are congenial for growth of dependence among children.

Among researchers who have studied the behaviour of the parents *vis-à-vis* repercussions of the same on children and who have reported results akin to the findings given above are, Miles (1945) Shobem (1949); Shapiro (1952); Block (1955); Croty (1957); Klebenoff (1957); Mann (1957); Mark (1963); Grams (1963); and Schaefer (1969). Their studies tended to support the view that democratic behaviour of parents brings self-control, self-determination and clarity of thought among children.

Emotional attitude (love/hostility) toward the child has been related to effective parental behaviour [Levy (1958); Moss & Robson (1968); Stern *et al.* (1969); Tulkin & Cohler (1973); Steward (1973)], and (b) Control and discipline of the child has been related to the degree and quality of controlling parental behaviour [Baumrind (1971); Backwith (1971) & Chamberlin (1974)]. Investigations have also linked these parental attitudes to child behaviours. Rejection and hostility have been held to be responsible for children's poor development [Bronfenbrenner (1961); Davids (1968). A positive affectionate attitude has been linked with more positive development [(Baldwin, Kalhern and Breese (1945); Lakin (1957); Stern *et al.* (1969)].

Tiedemann *et al.* (1981) analysed the relationship between type of parental behaviour and student disorders. Data were gathered from 246 fifth graders and their parents. One parental behaviour pattern that was found connected with several forms of behaviour-disorders at school, such as anxiety, lack of independence, rejection by others, disruptive classroom conduct and aggression, was deficiency in positive parental reinforcements together with an excess of punishment.

Cowan (1982) studied children's parental relationships and adjustment in 40 families. He found that children's adjustment was related to the amount of support and conflict between the parents and children's opportunity to maintain positive relationship with both parents.

Functions of parental attitude and behaviour antecedents in the development of child's personality was studied by Stevens (1983). The parental behaviour antecedents were maternal and paternal acceptance, psychological control and firm control, as reported by a sample of 44 college freshmen and as determined by the Children's Report of Parental Behaviour Inventory. The parental attitude antecedents were maternal authoritarianism and family disharmony, and parental democratic attitudes and detachment, as determined by the Parent Attitude Research Instrument. Self-reported child personality traits were nervous, depressive, active, social, expressive, responsive, sympathetic, subjective, dominant, hostile and self-disciplined as, determined by the Taylor Johnson Temperament Analysis. The maternal antecedents found to be most significantly related to all child personality traits except self-control were trust, acceptance, firm control, family harmony and moderate authoritarianism. The paternal antecedents found to be most significantly related to the child's personality traits were trust, acceptance and democratic attitudes.

Symonds (1939) in his study of 32 pairs of case studies consisting of one case that had been accepted by the parents and the other than had been rejected by them in each pair, found that the accepted child has every chance to develop into a well balanced and emotionally stable adult, while the rejected child is destined on the average to show strong aggressive traits of hostility and antagonism towards those with whom he might have dealings and to develop tendencies which may lead to delinquency.

Partridge (1939) has summarised statistical studies on the relationships between parents and adolescent boys and girls. He concluded that intimate and confidential relationships with parents, particularly with the mother, are definitely connected with good adjustments during adolescence. Maladjustment is much greater among the boys and girls who do not have harmonious, confidential relationships with parents; very severe parental discipline of children contributes heavily to adolescent maladjustments.

Martin (1943) examined 3,000 children below the age of thirteen (average age ten years, five months) by means of psychiatric interviews and observation of group activity. The purpose was to determine the relation of parental attitudes to the child's personality as revealed in group activities. This study revealed that all children have greater or lesser problems created by parental attitudes. Furthermore, it seemed clear that a child's behaviour was more directly related to the intensity of his problem than to its nature. Nervous behaviour, restlessness, tension and mannerisms seemed to be more related to over-protection and exploitation while anti-social expressions and behaviour such as swearing and stealing were more characteristic of the rejected and deprived child.

Zucker (1943) studied the relation of standards of behaviour and delinquency to the emotional attachment of children to their parents, using in addition to the case study materials, several projective techniques and extensive interviews. Comparisons were made of 25 delinquent and 25 non-delinquent boys. The study showed the lack of close emotional ties between most delinquent children. Open rejection by parents, broken homes and incessant quarrelling were typical of the delinquent homes.

Nihira, Yusin and Sinay (1975) studied parental behaviour as perceived by 86 adolescents aged 12 to 18 years in a crisis ward. In contrast to normal school age children, these adolescents viewed their parents as significantly more punitive, intrusive, restrictive, having higher demands for achievement for their children.

Rutkowski (1979) studied the relationship between adolescent alienation and an adolescent's perception of early parent-child relationships. The Adolescent's Alienation Index and Parent-Child Relations Questionnaire II were administered to 223 juniors in a diversified middle class suburban high school. Results of the study provided support for the conclusions that significant relationships do exist between adolescent alienation and the factors of love, rejection and affection.

Nunn (1983) examined the psycho-social adjustment of 633 school-aged children in grades 5 through 10. Of this group 56 per cent were male and 44 per cent female. Results revealed significant main effects upon psychosocial adjustment associated with family type, family process and gender. Specially youth from intact families demonstrated higher self-concepts, peer relations, state anxiety and trait anxiety scores. Psychosocial adjustments were more positive across all dimensions for children who perceived home in a positive fashion.

Sometimes the over-protection of children is an unconscious effort on the part of the parents to disguise their rejection of the child. However, children may sense this. Thorpe and Clark (1959) observed that over protection and/or over-direction on the part of a key person or key persons may cause behavioural immaturity in the child.

Home environment is of paramount importance for the psychological adjustment of the child. Parental rejection, over-protection, over-indulgence, severe punishment, nagging, criticism, faulty discipline results in behavioural problems in children (Symonds, 1938; Patridge, 1939; Martin, 1943; Zucker, 1943; Nihira *et al.* 1975; Chanpion, 1978; Rao and Sen, 1978; Rutkowski, 1979; Haigler, 1981; Tiedemanna *et al.*, 1981; Chong, 1982; Czarnik, 1984). Whereas children who are loved, accepted, nurtured, trusted who have close emotional ties with parents, who have parental affection, make harmonious adjustment (Watson, 1957; Stollenberger, 1969; Armentrout, 1972; Matteson, 1974; Growe, 1980; Gienapp, 1980; Rohner, 1980; Cowan, 1982; Stevens, 1983; Nunn, 1983; Shah, 1985).

STUDIES ON CHILD REARING PRACTICES AND MORAL JUDGEMENT

A number of investigations have been concerned with the relationship between parental child-rearing practices and moral development. Studies concerned with this field reveal that the use of affection and inductive discipline, rather than power assertion or love withdrawal as associated with greater reliance on internal standards and the use of intentionality in moral judgements. Hoffman and Saltzstein, 1967; Hoffman, 1970, 1971; Saltzstein, 1976. Holstein (1972) also found that parents who encourage the child's participation in discussion and decision-making were more likely to have children at higher levels of moral judgement. Haan, Smith and Block (1968) study on parental child-rearing practices reveal that parents of conventional subjects were perceived as insisting on rules, punishment and rewards whereas parents of post conventional subjects were perceived as allowing more autonomy, insisting on their own rights as parents and experiencing conflict with their children. Moreover it may be that the use of retrospective reports of child rearing practices might have been a source of bias because conventional subjects may be less likely to report conflict with their parents.

Furthermore due to the assumption that the mothers child-rearing practices are most important in the child's development, there has been relatively less interest in the role of father in the development of the child. However the theoretical models suggest that father is an important model for imitation (Bandura, 1969), a source of identification (Freud, 1933, 1965), means of providing opportunities for role making (Kohlberg, 1969), and might presumably affect moral development. Leahy (1981) observed that the acceptance and harmony in both mother and father appear to reflect the affection or nurturance. These parents appear to encourage mutuality within the family as well as nurturance and respect for the child's accomplishment. In families with autocratic ideology, discipline assumes a pre-dominant and pervasive role in the child-rearing process. Studies of Saltzstein, (1967), Hoffman (1970, 1971), reveal the use of affection and inductive discipline are covered with the relationship between parental child rearing practices and moral development.

Studies on child rearing practices by Arunodekar, Desai, and Singh (1973) in different socio-economic groups have shown that child rearing practices differed within the same culture groups. Mothers from higher socio-economic status were more rigid and severe in training their children than those from lower socio-economic group.

Goswami (1977) conducted a study on child rearing in Jianfia family; a socio-educational study of its beliefs, customs, practices and attitudes. The major objectives of the study were (1) to show how the Jianfias, both Christian and non-Christian had been following the old beliefs and customs in rearing their children, and how the modern civilisation had exerted influence in changing their age-old practices of child rearing (2) to point out lacunae in the methods of their child rearing in the matriarchal family and to make suggestion for their improvement. Fifteen villages surrounding Jowai town were chosen at random. Five families from each village and ten families in Jowai town formed the sample. This included Christian and non-Christian, and poor and rich families. The data were collected through interview and observation. The analysis of the data was mainly descriptive and analytical. Some of the major findings were as follows:

1. Majority of the parents were following the methods of child rearing which were based on superstitions.
2. Girls were considered as assets in the family while the boys were considered as the liabilities.
3. Child rearing was more a mother's job than father's.
4. Children did not have opportunity to develop habits of cleanliness from infancy and childhood.
5. Girls were trained more to shoulder responsibilities boys felt neglected.
6. Children were influenced by western values of the foreign missionaries. Changes had occurred due to changes in values and not because of religious beliefs.
7. Parents ignored the education of their children due to poverty.

Mathur and Shah (1963) describe child training methods as being roughly of two major categories: authoritarian and democratic. Authoritarian methods consist of strict rules and regulations with severe punishment for misbehaviour. Democratic methods, on the other hand, involve persuasion, explanation and reasoning with the child, with lenient forms of punishment. Variations in child-training methods are found within different social groups. Parents from rural areas are, on the whole, more authoritarian in their methods than urban parents. Social class differences in child training are significant and marked. Middle class parents are more exacting in their expectations. They begin training earlier, they supervise their children's activities more closely and they put greater emphasis on individual achievement than do parents from the lower class. With training, parents of the lower socio classes have been found to show greater leniency in their child care practices. The more conservative the parents, the more tolerant they are likely to be in their methods of training.

Aphole (1962) conducted a study on a Child in Home and School – a study of upbringing of children in Maharashtrian Hindu families in Poona. This was a sociological survey. One child below the age of ten in each of selected families from different wards of Poona with different economic, occupational, educational and cultural backgrounds was studied. Seven hundred such families were visited for the purpose of study. A questionnaire with a hundred and twenty statements regarding information about the family and the children, food habits, personal hygiene, health, education, recreation and miscellaneous other aspects constituted the main tool of research. The following were the major findings of study: (a) There was no uniformity in child rearing practices in the sampled families, (b) Highly educated advanced caste families belonging to rich and middle classes brought up their children in ways different from practices prevailing in uneducated or slightly educated poor scheduled caste families, (c) In the advanced families (1) children and carrying mothers were given special attention, (2) parents were keen to give the children some elementary education at home after which they were admitted to the preprimary school at proper age, (3) attention was paid to the extra curricular activities of the children and various recreational facilities were made available to them, (4) child care was shared by the male parent, and in joint families, by the other members of the family, (5) normally mild forms of punishment were used by the parents and severe punishment was resorted to only in case of extremely serious offences of children.

Watson (1957) reported the effects of permissive and restrictive controls of mothers upon child behaviour. He found that permissiveness helps in better socialisation and cooperation, more friendly feelings towards other children, higher degree of initiative and independence.

Stollenberger (1969) tested the assumption that the low delinquency rate among the Chinese Americans was due to their child rearing practices, their cultural values and their familial structure. Sixty-nine Chinese mothers were interviewed. In additional, the investigator participated in the daily life of China town for seven weeks. He concluded that the low delinquency rate may be due to nurturance, protection, intolerance of physical aggression, integrated family and good models of behaviour.

Seitz, Wehner and Henke (1970) investigated the relations among several personality traits and parental attitude towards child rearing. Subjects were forty-two 7-8 years old male students. Results showed a significant relationship between children's personality and parental child-rearing attitudes.

Armentrout (1972) examined sociometric popularity and children's reports of parental child rearing behaviours. Forty-eight boys and forty-eight girls in grades 4, 5 and 6 were selected from a large group of children on the basis of being high or low in sociometric popularity with their classmates. When their reports of perceived parental child rearing behaviours were compared, subjects high in popularity reported significantly greater acceptance by parents than did subjects low in popularity.

Kay (1975) stresses the importance of personalism in child-rearing practices. Parents who treat their children as persons worthy of consideration and respect rather than merely as occupants of an inferior status are more likely to help them to learn to respect others and show consideration for them.

He (1975) stresses the importance of moral flexibility, the ability to consider particular circumstances and special consideration surrounding a moral action or choice rather than applying blindly a rule that one has been taught. He suggest that it is only by being morally flexible that children can develop what he calls moral dynamism or creativity-something akin to what has been referred to earlier as moral autonomy.

Rigidity and flexibility in thinking are also reflected in children's moral conduct. Those accustomed to an authoritarian background are used to being told what to do and feel insecure outside such a framework. They seem to prefer authority to autonomy and are reluctant to make their own moral choices because of the degree of uncertainty involved. They are more concerned with particular instances than children who have learnt to be flexible in their moral thinking and to look for a general principle underlying particular rules and regulations.

Psychologists have always taken keen interest in the study of child-rearing practices and related this to the development of specific personality traits (Symonds, 1939; Radkey, 1946; Brapenbvenner, 1953; Betleheim, 1952; Read, 1945; Slohen, 1949; Harris, Gough and Maitin, 1950; Shapiro, 1952; Klebanoff, 1957; Mann, 1957). The modern dynamic psychology lays heavy emphasis on the socialisation process, the process by which an individual grows from a dependent infant into an independent and dependable adult. The infant's life after birth is dependent upon the child-rearing practice. Because the first source of nutrition and the child's security, comfort and survival depend upon the mother's care. Studies like Symonds (1938), Levy (1942), Baldwia (1945), Kanner (1948), Shoben (1949), Sears (1957), Hess (1970), Maccoby *et al.* (1975), Blehar and Others (1977), Harrington, *et al.* (1978), Rohner (1980-81), Faizunnisa (1965, 1967), Iffat Unnisa (1965), Nalini Devi (1967), Alit Rama (1967), Warty (1970), Pariera and Tirtha (1972), Patel (1965), Fictor (1975), Sidhana and Sinha (1975), Choudhari (1975), Hussain (1970), Bhogle (1978-79), Saraswati (1979), Singh (1981), Chauhan and Tiwari (1981) have pointed out the effects of different maternal attitudes on the personality development of the child.

STUDIES ON EMOTIONAL MATURITY AND MORAL JUDGEMENT

Mast-cruce (1976) conducted a study on the inter relationship of critical thinking, empathy and social interest with moral judgement. The objectives of the study were to explore the aspect of morality which according to some therapists, is an important variable in mental health, that is moral judgement and also to determine the contributions made to moral decisions by the variables critical thinking, empathy and social interest. The sample consisted of 108 volunteers enrolled in courses in the Department of Guidance and Educational Psychology at Southern Illinois University. The scores for the subjects were admitted to a multiple regression analysis. The findings of the study were (1) Social interest, as measured in this study is not a useful predictor of moral judgement (2) Critical thinking and empathy are components of moral decision-making. The study has also shown that the development of moral judgement is related to many factors like age, sex, socio-economic status, empathy, ethnic factors and so on. They have also shown that programmes may be developed to inculcate moral judgement capacity among children.

Fefis (1970) investigated the relationship between predictive ability, empathy, intelligence and sex to moral judgement in adolescents. The subjects were 39 high school students aged 17 years of age studying in 9th grade level. The tools that were administered were DIT, Predictive Ability Test, Otis Lennon Mental Ability Test and Empathy Scale of the California Psychological Inventory. Correlations between predictive ability, empathy, intelligence, sex and moral judgement scales did not reach a statistically significant level. When classed by sex it was found that the correlation of 0.654 for empathy and moral judgement was significant for males at the 0.05 level.

Lal (1968) conducted a comparative study on emotional stability of mentally superior and average adolescents. The study was confined to higher secondary schools of Madhya Pradesh. Emotional stability was assessed by the Personality Inventory by Lal and the Roschach Ink Blot Test. The average and superior pupils were equated on the basis of their socio-economic status using the Kuppuswamy's Socio-economic Status Scale. The important findings of the study showed emotional stability increased with age in the superior group, it deteriorated with age in the average group. Both the groups were ruled by immediate need for gratification. The average group showed a more withdrawing type of behaviour. Both groups were almost similar in their relationship with others in society.

Emotional control or stability is one of the seven important indicators of mental health (Scott, 1968). It affects learning in the school context. Its absence impairs performance in situations which require flexibility and adaptability; it leads to anxiety, feelings of inferiority and guilt (Frandsen, 1961). Douglas (1964) reports that the attitude of the pupils to their school work is deeply affected by the level of their emotional stability.

Bose (1960) conducted a study on the personality patterns of a group of institutionalised boys with a view to understanding certain emotional factors leading to problem behaviour. The sample comprised various categories of offenders belonging to different parts of the country, in the age range seven to eighteen years, with an average age of 12.8 years. The tools used for collecting data were observations, interviews, consultations of relevant records and administration of Alexander's Pass a Long Test, Goodenough's Draw-a-Man Test, Word Association Test and Thematic Appreciation Test. The important findings of the study were (1) Loss of support and security, denial of home affection, deprivation of material benefits had turned them into wayward vagrants, capable of doing mischief of any kind or degree, (2) Mentally they showed lack of persistency in efforts, concentration, lack of perception of relationships and also of clear vision of gradual steps involved in an operation, (3) They had a very slow development of concept formation and still slower speed of performing a task, (4) The boys were low in intellectual capacities, (5) The common theme of their stories centered around deprivation, lack of love, conflict of desires, offence and punishment, dominance, escape, family trends, etc., (6) The development of ego in these boys was disturbed.

STUDIES ON PERSONALITY TRAITS AND MORAL JUDGEMENT

Zamean (1982) conducted a study of social, religious and moral values of students of XI and their relationship with moral character traits and personality adjustment. The investigation was of the survey type. The sample consisted of 560 students. The tools of the study were the Value Scale and Character Trait Questionnaire, both prepared by the investigator. The values of test-retest and split-half reliabilities were significant. The major findings of the study were – (1) The religious values had the greatest influence on character traits and lowest on personality adjustment. It also implied that the development and strengthening of a healthy social, moral and religious value systems among students should be a very important function of the secondary schools which would help in solving problems of student unrest and discipline.

Kumar (1972), studied the social climate in school and characteristics of pupils, i.e., student behaviour in terms of personal social adjustment, value orientation and attitude towards certain educational objects and scholastic achievement. The criterion variables examined in the study included personality characteristics like activity, hypomanic temperament, emotional instability and introversion. The non-governmental and co-educational high schools in Gujarat state, in existence for at least ten years served as the population. Observations in criterion behaviours were collected from students of class X of selected schools and statistical analysis was carried out on school means to examine the effect of social climate in schools on student behaviour. The finding suggest that different social climates have differential effects on certain aspects of students behaviour. Personality characteristics such as emotional instability depressive tendency, moral values, activity and introversion differentiate between climate groups and to a lesser extent, characteristics such as hypomanic temperament and dominance tend to differentiate them. Among the climates the schools with open climate, tend to show better personal adjustment of pupils than the other groups of climate. The results of the present study point to a possibility of basic causal link between climate characteristics of pupil variables.

Mathew (1971) studied the personality patterns of college students specialising in different fields. The study was to find out whether there were significant differences in values, temperament and vocational interests among college students specialising in different fields. The tools used in the study were three personality inventories, AVL study of values, and the Guilford-Zimmerman Temperament Survey. The conclusion is that significant differences in values, temperament and vocational interests exist among college students specialising in different fields in Kerala.

Gupta (1970) made a comparative study of the personality characteristics of high and low achievers. The Jalota Group Test of Mental Ability was administered to 330 IX class students with a view to keep intelligence constant in the study. Their status of academic achievement was determined from their half-yearly examination marks. The sample finally drawn consisted of 56 boys and 28 girls in the high achiever group and equal numbers in the low achievers group. Personality Trait Inventory was used as a tool for collecting the relevant data. The study has resulted in the following conclusions: (1) Industry, persistence and intensive work raises the level of academic achievement; (2) Positive and healthy attitude towards moral values (especially in girls) raises achievement; (3) Paranoid and depressive tendencies affect the students' (specially the low achieving families) scholastic progress adversely; (4) Emotional maladjustment lowers scholastic progress; (5) Introversion slows down progress (especially in low achieving males).

Kakkar (1964) studied the relationship between personality structure, pscyho-social structure and adjustment, complications of mental hygiene and educational guidance. Also the influence of the problems on learning efficiency. It was conducted on a random sample of 75 girls and 75 boys of class XI of nine higher secondary schools of Allahabad. The tools used in the study were Raven's Progressive Matrices Test, Asthana's Adjustment Inventory, Personality Inventory prepared by Allahabad Bureau of Psychology and Rorschach Ink Blot Test. Data was processed through chi-square and correlational techniques. Results showed that 43 per cent cases had serious adjustment problems. The school area posed the greatest number of problems, while in the home the adolescents were overdependent on parents. Boys were more aggressive and curious about the new knowledge while girls were shy, withdrawn and nervous. In social areas, problems like how to be popular, how to get along with others worried the adolescents. The data also revealed that adjustment and personality problems increased with an increase in the level of intelligence. The school problems of Indian adolescents were more serious than those of their counterparts in U.S.A.

Raniji (1968) conducted a study to analyse the concept of personality in the educational thought of Mahatma Gandhi. To have a coherent view, 4,300 statements of Gandhi pertaining to personality and education were analysed. In Gandhi's thought, a special stress on the development of the self is predominant. According to him the aim of life as well as education is self realisation and education should develop the self which is an in important component of personality. The permanent basis of personality is the universal self which is a synonym of truth force, life force, love force, goodness, knowledge, beauty, peace and pure delight. Thus the educational activities in Gandhi's thought exercise their healthy impact in the three components of personality–self, mind and body and promote the healthy harmonious development of the whole personality of the educand.

STUDIES ON SOCIO-ECONOMIC STATUS AND MORAL JUDGEMENT

Evidence shows that there are in fact social class differences that affect children's moral development. Studies by Sears *et al.* (1957), Kohn (1958), Kohlberg (1966), Kay (1968) and Bull (1969), to mention but a few, all suggest that children from families of higher social status show greater maturity in moral judgement than those from lower social class backgrounds.

There are several possible reasons for these differences. Firstly, it has been suggested that children from higher status families tend to be future-oriented. Parents offer them guidance in advance so that they are encouraged to consider the consequences of their actions. Conversely, parents of lower social status tend to punish after a misdemeanour, so that their children are more likely to be concerned with the immediate present. Linked with this is the practices in higher status of families of deferring gratification; children are thus further helped to consider long-term consequences and, it is claimed are less likely to break promises, tell lies or steal out of pure expediency and consideration only of present circumstances. Furthermore, as Henderson and Bernstein (1969) demonstrate, middle class parents spend more time answering children's questions, giving them reasons why they are expected to behave in certain ways and explaining why they consider some behaviour morally unacceptable. Children from such families are thus more likely to understand reasons offered to them and to formulate their own at an early age than those from lower status families.

Kalra (1978), conducted a study on the moral judgement in children belonging to different mental and socio-economic levels. The objectives of the study were to (1) Construct a tool for measuring the level of development of moral judgement of children, (2) To find out the difference, if any, in the levels of moral judgement in the children of different mental levels, (3) To find out whether there was any difference in the levels of moral judgement in the different socio-economic levels. The tools used were Standard Progressive Matrices, Socio-economic Status Scale and a Moral Judgement Scale developed by the investigator. The sample comprised of 1000 girls from fifteen schools of the Western Zone of Delhi. The findings of the study were (1) Intelligence was positively related with the level of moral judgement at all the three levels of socio-economic status (2) Socio-economic status was positively related with the level of moral judgement at all levels of intelligence.

Hilton (1978) attempted to study the relationship between interpersonal trust, socio-economic status and intelligence and moral judgement. The study revealed a positive correlation between the dependent variable moral judgement and socio-economic status of students.

Helen (1973) investigated relationship between moral judgement and age, intelligence and three levels of socio-economic status. A significant and direct relationship was postulated between socio-economic status as related to opportunities for enriching one's social experience and therefore, to moral judgement. Kohlberg also demonstrated a positive relationship between socio-economic status and moral judgement at two levels, low and middle. This study included a third level (upper socio-economic status). A 2 x 3 x 2 analysis of variance design was used. Tools used were

California Tests of Basic Skills, modified Hollingshed Index for measuring socio-economic status and moral maturity score was derived from open ended questions asked of the subject after Kohlberg's Moral Dilemmas were read to the subjects. Sample consisted of 120 subjects randomly selected from local public schools. It was found that the intelligence was directly related to moral judgement and increase in socio-economic status was related to increase in moral judgement.

Mohundro (1976) attempted to determine a relationship between Kohlberg's stages of reasoning expressed in the justification of values and with the value hierarchy. Sex and socio-economic status were also studied. Sample consisted of 60 students selected randomly and the tools used were modified Rokeach Value Survey-Form D and an Interview Schedule. ANOVA was used to analyse the obtained data. It was found that socio-economic status was related to the stages of moral reasoning and value positions.

Johnston (1981) conducted a study to determine whether selected children's stories can be utilised to increase scores on Kohlberg's moral development scale for 6th grade samples. Tools used were Moral Judgement Interviews and reading a story and identifying the moral dilemma. Statistical techniques used to analyses the data were t-test and two-way ANOVA. The findings revealed no sex difference in moral growth. But there was a significant difference mean gain score changes of the low socio-economic group and the middle socio-economic groups, with latter group showing greater gain. Socio-economic status was found to be a significant factor in moral growth. This study revealed that there was a significant correlation between socio-economic status and moral judgement.

Lewis (1982) compared the moral development of gifted students with the moral development of regular students. The independent variables were sex, age, socio-economic status and ability psychometrically defined. The tools used were: 1) 'P' score from the DIT (Moral Development Test), 2) Inventory of Piaget's Development Task, 3) Socio-economic Status was measured by the Home Index. A sample of 120 students consisting of 60 boys and 60 girls were drawn from an urban and rural high school. An equal number of subjects were selected from grades 10, 11, 12 for a cell size of 10. Three way analysis of variance and Pearson product moment correlation was employed to analyse the data.

The findings indicated a positive correlation between cognitive and moral development and between cognitive development and socio-economic status. Gifted students were found to be significantly different from regular students in socio-economic status. To look more closely at the influence of the socio-economic status on both moral development and cognitive development, the sample of 120 was divided into two groups according to socio-economic status. One group was a group of high socio-economic status and the other was a group of low socio-economic status. A significant difference was found between the groups with regard to cognitive development but not for moral judgement.

Evans (1980), Gongre (1981) and Johnson (1979) found no relationship regarding socio-economic status and stages of moral development and moral judgement.

STUDIES ON SEX DIFFERENCES AND MORAL JUDGEMENT

Soni (1984) conducted a study on moral judgement of school going children of rural area of Delhi belonging to different castes and sexes. The objective of the study were (1) To construct and develop a moral judgement scale which could be used to find the level of development of moral judgement of school going children of rural area of Delhi, (2) To find out whether there was any real difference in moral judgement of children belonging to different castes and (3) To find whether there was any difference in moral judgement of boys and girls. Coloured progressive matrices to measure intelligence and a moral judgement test were the tools used. The major findings of the study were –

1. In both the sexes as well as in the combined group each of the caste groups – Brahmins, *Vaishyas* and *Kshatriyas* had done better than the *shudras.*
2. In all the caste groups as well as in the whole group, girls were better than boys in moral judgement.

Devendra and Mishra (1981) conducted a study on development of moral judgement in Indian children. The sample consisted of 120 Indian children of 6-11 years of age. Analysis of data involved 3 x 2 x 2 factorial experimental design with 3 age levels – 6-7, 8-9, 10-11 years, two sex groups (Male and Female) and two levels of economic status (high and low). The major findings were, there was significant main effect of age. Also age x sex and age and economic status interaction yielded significant effects. The interaction of the three independent factors were also found to be significant. It was also concluded that although the capacity for moral judgement increases with age, the pattern is significantly mediated by factors of sex and socio-economic status.

Bush (1981) investigated the validity of Kohlberg's measure of moral reasoning from a role identification stand point. The study proposed that respondents will vary in their staging relative to their ability to emphasize with moral dilemmas. Specifically, the sex of the protagonist in the dilemma and the role relevance of the dilemma were manipulated to increase empathy. Tools used in the study were – Defining Issues Test (DIT) and Alternate Dilemma Questionnaire (ADQ). Sample consisted of 120 seniors randomly selected from a class of 236 were administered the ADQ and the DIT. The findings revealed that males and females staged significantly higher on the ADQ than on the DIT and males and females were staged essentially the same on the ADQ. This study has given support to other research findings that males do not posses higher moral reasoning than females. In fact, it is possible, that adolescent females have a greater sensitivity to moral dilemma.

Kipust (1983) compared educated boys to girls of 9th and 11th grade, for moral development and self-concept and found that the moral development scores of girls were significantly higher than those of boys for the overall sample and for the 9th grade level. But no such significant difference was found at the 11th grade level.

Schunrer (1976) investigated moral reasoning in young adults and also examined the interaction of various personality characteristics with attained level of moral reasoning, across and between sexes. Samples consisted of 50 female and 50 male college undergraduates in education, between the age 19 and 25 years. Instruments used to collect the data were the Kohlberg Moral Judgement Scale, the Morlowe-Crown Scale, the Rotter I.E., Scale and the California Personality Inventory. The study revealed differences in favour of males over females in the attained level of moral reasoning. The reasoning of young women were more pragmatic, stereotyped to immature. The reasoning of men were more vigorous, autonomous and independent. Certain personality variables were significantly correlated with the moral maturity score.

Researches by Maccoby (1966), Anastaci (1966) and Horner (1972) had demonstrated that females scored equally well or slightly above males on a number of developmental measures at an early age but female's score tended to stabilize prematurely during the adolescent period. In terms of moral reasoning, proportionately more females remained at the conventional level than males and lesser percentage reached the post-conventional level (Kohlberg and Turiel, 1971; Hunn, 1971; Holstein, 1973). One explanation for this difference was that limitations were imposed on female's growth by social conventions and behavioural expectations.

Wright and Cox (1967) conducted a study on the relationship between moral judgement and religious belief in a sample of English adolescents. The major objectives of the study were to (1) Examine the degree of severity of moral judgement on a number of behavioural items, and (2) To analyse the relationship between moral judgement and various indices of religious belief and practice. The sample consisted of 2,276 pupils 49.6% were boys and 50.4% girls drawn from 6th forms of 96 grammar schools in England. The technique used for collection of data were questionnaires. The major findings of the study were (1) On nearly all items, girls were more severe in their judgements than boys, (2) Age, subject studied and experience of co-education were not found to be related to moral judgement (3) Consistency indices of religiosity were found to be related to severity of moral judgement and (4) The more ascetic the moral issue, the stronger the association with religious belief and practice.

Banon (1982) conducted a study on sex differences in parental press at several socio-economic levels. The study was conducted to know the parental involvement and their contribution to the education of the child. The investigator prepared Parental Press Inventory, Socio-economic Status Questionnaire, Achievement test in English, Achievement test in general knowledge and Achievement test in arithmetic. For the analysis of data, the statistical techniques used were critical ratio, product moment correlation, partial correlation, three way ANOVA and multiple regression. The major findings of the study were (1) The distribution of scores of boys and girls in all the five areas (educational, social, physical, emotional and moral) of parental press showed lack of symmetry, (2) The girls secured better points in educational and physical areas whereas boys exhibited better scores in the emotional and moral areas (3) Sex, locality and SES did not affect the parental press scores, (4) The emotional, educational and moral areas of parental press appeared to make major contribution in the prediction of academic achievement of boys whereas in the case of girls, moral, social and educational areas of parental press seemed to contribute much in the prediction of academic achievement, (5) For both the groups moral press played a dominating role among the five areas of parental press.

Gupta (1977) studied individual differences in value pattern and personality type of the school going adolescents. A sample of 400 boys and 400 girls were taken from the secondary schools of Eastern U.P. They were administered Joshi's General Mental Ability Test, and the Typological Structure Test developed by Dwivedi on the lines of Shelden's classification of personality. The t-test was used for analysis of data. The major findings of the study was boys and girls differed significantly in their values.

Gopalaiah (1981) conducted a study on moral judgement in children. The sample consisted of 60 boys and 60 girls belonging to 6 different age groups with equal number in each which constituted the subjects for this investigation. The technique used was interview technique and a socio-economic scale was administered. Analysis of data involved chi-square technique.

The major findings were:

1. Between the ages of 7 and 17 years a vivid development was traced in moral judgement. As age increased the level of moral judgement reached higher and higher level.
2. The moral judgement did not depend on sex.
3. The high achievers were characterised by higher level of moral judgement of socionomy and autonomy.
4. The average achievers had equal levels of judgement among heteronomy, socionomy and autonomy.
5. The low achievers were characterised by heteronomy levels of judgement.
6. There was no difference between the levels of moral judgement of children and their religious background.

7. There was no difference between the moral judgement and socio-economic status of children.

Kenvin (1981) conducted a study to determine the relationship among systematic secular value education, programmed religious education and secular general education in terms of level of moral judgement. Sample consisted of 3 groups of high school students, each of which included 15 females and 15 males. The DIT was administered to the students as a pretest and post-test. Techniques used to analyse the data were two-way ANOVA and t-test. The findings indicated that there was no significant difference between the levels on which female and male high school students make moral judgement.

Toai Ton (1978) investigated the relation of age, sex and adult authority figure to moral judgement in Vietnamese immigrant children. A sample of 144 Vietnamese immigrant children of both sexes from grade 1, 4 and 5 of 17 primary schools in Virginia were selected to participate in the study'. These children were tested with a moral reasoning instrument and an accompanying objective pictorials punishment scale. It was found that there was no sex difference despite the traditional sex dichotomy in Vietnamese culture.

Researches done by Siefering (1981), Fifis (1978), Benninga (1976) and Johnson (1981) also indicated that there is no significant sex difference in moral judgement scores of students.

Dockstander (1979) made a comparative study of developmental sex differences in moral reasoning. The purpose of this study was threefold:

1. To determine if there was a significant difference between the levels of development of females and males at the 7th and 11th grades.
2. To ascertain if a moral education intervention of 12 weeks significantly stimulated the moral reasoning of

7th and 11th grade students compared to control groups and

3. To determine if the intervention significantly stimulated the moral reasoning of 7th and 11th females.

The findings of this study showed no significant difference between males and females in the levels of moral development at the 7th and 11th grade, using the Rest Defining Issues Test. At the 7th grade level there was a significant difference at the 0.05 level between the moral reasoning of female experimental students and female control group students but no such difference was shown at the 11th grade level.

STUDIES ON TYPE OF MANAGEMENT AND MORAL JUDGEMENT

Rao and Mehta (1979), in their study on 1,120 boys of 23 schools, found that the home and school are important and significant factors in children's authoritarianism, secular outlook, modernity and out-group prejudices. The privately managed schools appeared to enhance authoritarianism, reduce secularism and modernity and promote social prejudice in children.

Du Freez (1977) conducted a study on the moral judgement and religious problems and attitudes as expressed by students in 7th day adventist academics in the US and Canada. The sample consisted of 1920 students chosen by a stratified random method from all enrolled in 7th day adventist academy in the US and Canada. Data collection was done by a responsible person designated by each school principal. Chi-square and ANOVA were the statistical methods used in the analysis of the data. The findings of the study were students are dissatisfied with the help that the academy and church, through faculty, staff and teachers are giving them with their personal problems. But they are satisfied with the spiritual, educational, social as well as recreational activities provided to meet their needs and interests.

Gorman (1979) conducted a study on the relationship between moral judgement and religious knowledge scores of Catholic high school boys of 9th and 12th grades. The Moral Inventory Test was administered to a sample of 190 boys. Analysis of data involved correlation coefficient. The findings of the study showed that religious knowledge scores of 12th grade students were significantly correlated to the moral judgement scores.

A study was conducted by Wallin (1978) on learning disabilities, religious treatment and moral judgement of junior high school boys. The sample consisted of 48 Jewish 7th and 8th grade male youngsters of secular schools and religious schools in New York city. The technique used for data collection was Rests Defining Issue Test. The major findings were – normal students had significantly higher DIT scores than learning disabled students. The cognitive development may be related to moral judgement in so far as learning disabled youngsters. The higher DIT scores on the part of youngsters attending religious schools indicated that Jewish training may be effective in fostering the development of moral judgement.

The objectives of the study by Gupta (1984) were to find out the stages of moral development of school children and also to study the moral reasoning of children of various age groups. The tools for the data collection were Moral Reasoning Scale, Moral Dilemmas Scale and the Personal Data Sheet. The following were the main findings of the study. Reasoning was used by the children at the age of 12, the use of which declined sharply with the increase in age. As the child matured, he used fewer and fewer arguments of reward and punishment. The children from co-educational schools showed lower reformatory zeal in comparison to the children from non co-educational schools.

A study was conducted by Stoop (1980) on the relation between religious education and the process of maturity through the developmental stages of moral judgement. The sample consisted of 390 high school students participating in 4 different types of formal religious education. The objectives of the study was to determine the effect of religious education on the cognitive developmental construct of moral reasoning. The tool used for data collection was Rests' Defining Issue Test. The analysis of data involved multiple regression analysis. Major findings of the study were that the hypothesised interaction between grade and school on 4 stages and four scores calculated by F test yielded an F ratio of 2.08 which was not significant. Conservative Christian religious education would appear to stimulate stage 4 moral reasoning causing an early acceleration to this stage. There appears to be a relation between the process of maturity in moral development and some forms of religious education. Religious education would appear to stimulate principles of moral reasoning as measured by the scores.

Conclusions

The following are some of the salient inferences stemming from the review of available related literature and studies.

1. Parental behaviour, parental disciplinary practices and parental relationship with the child is a powerful determinant of child's moral judgement and behaviour. Studies in this pertinent area have all highlighted the importance of the role of parents in more mature moral development, judgement and behaviour.
2. It is apparent that child rearing practices have tremendous impact on moral development and moral judgement of children. Flexible child rearing practices are advocated. Further indepth studies need to undertaken in this vital area.
3. The place of emotions and emotional maturity has been largely ignored by researchers, though it has been clearly accepted that emotions may well be the most important

factor in the moral behaviour of most people. Research studies are by far few and limited and warrants attention in this direction.

4. The review of studies on effect of personality traits on moral judgement of children are also limited and there is a dearth of studies in this pertinent area which necessitates further studies.
5. Researches on the effect of sex differences on moral judgement show inconsistent findings. Studies by Schruner (1976) and Maccoby (1966) arrived at contradictory results the former found males more prone to mature judgement while the latter found female slightly better than males in their moral judgement. Studies by Gopaliah (1981), Kenvin (1981), Toai Ton (1978), Seifung (1981), Fefis (1978), Benimings (1976) and Johnson (1981) found no significant sex differences in the moral judgement of male and female students. Further researches are needed to clarify the inconsistencies in research findings.
6. Socio-economic differences did have a significant impact on moral judgement of children where high socio-economic status students showed greater maturity in moral judgement than those from lower socio-economic status.
7. Last but not the least a few studies on effect of type of management on moral judgement clearly indicate its relation to moral judgement of children. The paucity of research in the areas of emotional maturity, personality traits and type of management has helped the investigator to identify the gaps and weaknesses in the studies reviewed. The present investigation is a humble attempt at trying to bridge this gap.

CHAPTER III

METHODOLOGY

In this chapter the terms and concepts used in the study have been operationally defined. The discussion of variables have also been included in the study in order to establish the rationality for having chosen them. Hypotheses have been stated for empirical validation. The procedures followed in selecting the sample and the tools used for data collection have been presented. Finally, the statistical techniques used for data analysis have been explained.

The purpose of this investigation was to study the moral judgement of students as related to parental behaviour, child rearing practices, emotional maturity and personality traits. It was also the intention of the investigator to find out whether differences in the independent variables namely parental behaviour, child rearing practices, emotional maturity, personality traits, socio-economic status, sex and type of management would account for significant differences in the moral judgement of students. The investigator further attempted to find out the main and interaction effects of the independent variables on the dependent variable, moral judgement of students.

3.1. OPERATIONAL DEFINITIONS

Under this heading the terms and concepts operationally defined are moral judgement, parental behaviour, child rearing practices, emotional maturity and personality traits.

OPERATIONAL DEFINITION OF MORAL JUDGE-MENT

Moral judgement in this study has been defined in terms of five dimensions.

Honesty

It is a strong will and the ability to live up to the intellectual convictions and to act thereafter in terms of that knowledge.

Truthfulness

Truthfulness is that dimension of moral judgement where an individual reveals the true happenings inspite of knowing that he would be punished if the act is against the expectation of the society or an individual.

Non-violence

It is that dimension of moral judgement where an individual is harmed by others, but he does not harm them in turn. Rather he tries to impress them and make them follow the peaceful path by his harmless behaviour.

Obedience

This dimension of moral judgement measures the behaviour of an individual who has to follow certain rules and regulations, by not involving either himself in risk or troubling others, thereby creating a pleasant social atmosphere.

Justice

An individual who seeks justice always wants the rewards to the extent of his behaviour being correct and not out of sympathy or otherwise. He does not mind exposing his negative behaviour when he does not deserve any rewards or being rewarded out of some chance factor.

Thus the five dimensions of moral judgement indicate the extent an individual is capable of judging the behaviour of himself and of others in terms of moral and ethical expectation with in the society.

PARENTAL BEHAVIOUR

In the present study the definition operationalised by Dr. Uma Saxena and Dr. N.K. Saxena (1977) for parental behaviour (mother form) has been used. Parental behaviour is defined as the rapport between the child and the parents which is made visible from the observed behaviour of the child to judge whether the child has got good training from the parents or not. How a child perceives the behaviour of his parents towards him is very important. Children's report of their parental behaviour plays a very important role in the personality development. Children's home adjustment, anxiety, security, insecurity, frustration and feeling of adequacy are very much influenced by how they perceive their parental behaviour particularly the mother.

Parental behaviour (mother form) in this study is defined in terms of Acceptance, Child Centeredness, Possessiveness, Rejection, Control, Enforcement, Positive Involvement, Intrusiveness, Control Through Guilt, Hostile Control, Inconsistent Discipline, Non-Enforcement, Acceptance of Individuation, Lack of Discipline, Instilling Persistent Anxiety, Hostile Detachment, Withdrawal of Relations and Extreme Autonomy. A mother may be very warm in her relationship with her child, but her child may perceive her as cold. There may be communication gap between actual feeling and attitudes of the mothers toward their children and the latter's perception towards them.

CHILD REARING PRACTICES

Child Rearing means 'Socialisation'. The process by which a child, born into a given society, becomes a social being. It is the interaction between the parents and their children. Smart and Smart held that the unfolding of an individual's potentials is determined by the type of the environment he is surrounded with. Child rearing includes much more than providing a child food, shelter and clothing which are basic for growth. It has to be provided opportunities for the realisation of its potentialities with love and affection. It has been observed that lack of love can hamper the physical, mental and emotional growth of the child.

Child rearing practices differ from culture to culture and also among different groups within the same culture. They are influenced among other things, by the educational level, economic condition and traditional value system of the family. Religious and regional differences have also been found to exist in the child rearing patterns in India.

Child rearing practices in this study is defined in terms of both child-rearing practices and child-rearing attitudes, which include both Mother form and Father form. Father form is defined in terms of five factors (1) Comfort and Encouragement, (2) Control and Supervision, (3) Acceptance and Harmony, (4) Ambivalence about child's autonomy and (5) Does not allow Independence whereas mother form is defined in terms of 6 factors, namely, (1) Comfort and Encouragement, (2) Acceptance and Harmony, (3) Control Sex and Aggression: Authoritarian, (4) Punitive and Controlling, (5) Intrusiveness and (6) Maintain Boundaries between Child and Others.

EMOTIONAL MATURITY

It is operationally defined in the present study as the perception of an individual of his self-knowledge, self-confidence, acceptance of reality, self-control, social adjustment and consistency. These six components have been operationally defined as follows:

i) ***Self Knowledge***: A person who is emotionally mature normally knows to a great extent his abilities, capacities and potentialities. This awareness helps him to react to outside situations in a more mature manner. A person who does not possess adequate knowledge, about himself is likely to act in an immature way. The awareness of one's own abilities and dispositions is operationally defined as self-knowledge in the present study.

ii) ***Self Confidence***: A person by virtue of his potentialities and successful experiences develops confidence in himself especially when he receives proper appreciation for good responses. Thus, he is able to think that he can make his own decisions and to accept the consequences thereof. He is likely to resolve his own conflicts. In other words, this self-confidence is a characteristic of an emotionally mature person.

iii) ***Acceptance of Reality***: An emotionally mature person is more likely to give due consideration to the reality of a situation and understand it in the light of his social and cultural background. This acceptance of reality is another characteristic of a mature person.

iv) ***Self Control***: The self control of an emotionally mature person manifests itself in controlling his anger, fear, jealousy, etc. in situations which may provoke him. His behaviour therefore, will be in a socially approved manner. Self-control is considered as a desirable trait of an emotionally mature person.

v) ***Social Adjustment***: In modern society where fast changes are taking place in social and cultural values, the generation gap is seen more prominently. Secondly, there are gaps in the social acceptance and rejection models. An emotionally mature person is able to understand the gaps and continuously strives for adjustment in various situations both with regard to conformity and innovative practices.

vi) ***Consistency***: An emotionally mature person does not exhibit erratic behaviour. Even in stress he is able to maintain a mental balance. He does not impulsively decide either to quit or to fight. He can tolerate frustrations and guide himself in such a manner by the integrity of his personality. One can predict his behaviour because of a high level of consistency in his reactions.

PERSONALITY TRAITS

Introversion and Extroversion

Introversion is the opposite inward turning tendency that makes a person sensitive to his own feelings and experiences and causes him to direct his efforts toward understanding them. Extroversion is defined as the kind of outward orientation that makes a person highly aware of what is going on around him and causes him to direct his energy towards objects and people outside himself. The intermediate version of introversion-extroversion is called ambiversion.

3.2. VARIABLES OF THE STUDY

Dependent Variable Moral Judgement, *viz.*, Honesty, Truthfulness, Non-violence, Obedience, Justice

Independent Variables- 1. Parental Behaviour 2. Child Rearing Practices 3. Emotional Maturity 4. Personality Traits 5. Socio-Economic Status 6. Sex 7. Type of School Management

3.3. DISCUSSION OF VARIABLES

MORAL JUDGEMENT

Moral Judgement is an aspect of intellectual activity. The study of moral judgement inevitably leads one to consider the relatively clear and comprehensible activity of human thought. Here the individual is primarily involved in cognitive activity. He is applying his mind to a moral problem, just as he would solve a logical problem and reach a decision by purely intellectual means, so he applies the same mental apparatus to a moral problem and reaches a decision by almost exactly the same process. Intelligence relates strongly to moral judgement and behaviour as it does to a great many other dimensions of human functioning. The disagreement about the role of intelligence in morality turns on the issue of how much part intelligence has, and whether high intellectual capacity ensures high moral development.

Mischel and Mischel surveyed a variety of studies showing a clear relation between cognitive competence and general adequacy of social functioning. Maturity on Piagetian moral judgement was found to be positively correlated with intelligence and dishonest behaviour was found to be negatively related. On the basis of such data Aronfreed and Mischel and Mischel accent the role of sheer cognitive power is the operation of conscience and question whether children comparable in general cognitive capacity would show any significant variation in principles of conscience.

Is conscience no more than a matter of intelligence. Behavioural evidence shows that something else is involved as suggested by Burton's (1946) review of studies showing for example, that the relation between intelligence and honesty declines or disappears when the context is non-academic or when the risk of getting caught is low. Turning to the realm of judgement, one finds that while high Intelligence children do better than low Intelligence subjects on most Piaget tests of moral judgement, for some dimensions the reverse is true. Cognitive development theories such as Kohlberg and Selman have offered a way of clarifying the intelligence-morality relation. A given stage of cognitive development is necessary but not sufficient condition for the parallel moral stage. The relevant data are generally supportive, 93 per cent of all 5 to 7 year olds who passed a moral reasoning task at Kohlberg's stage (which involves primitive social reciprocity) passed a correspondence task of logical reciprocity, where as fifty two per cent of the children who passed the logical task did not pass the moral test. The necessary but not sufficient relationship appears to hold at the higher levels as well. All adolescents and adults who score at stages, five or six are capable of formal reasoning on Piaget's pendulum and correlation problems, but many persons who are formal operational on these logical problems fail to show any moral reasoning at the highest, post-conventional stages.

The research, then appears to be confirming a common intuition, being smart and being moral are not the same. Cognitive powers may be needed for principled moral thought, but it is not enough. History is full of examples of how human intelligence can be turned to great evil, the understanding of which stands the next critical challenge to a science of morality. Durkheim, for example, found hardly any evidence at all that a child's intelligence was correlated with the level of his moral judgement.

Most challenging and controversial is that view that moral judgement and specifically moral reasoning, involves the child's passage through a series of successive stages characterised by increasing degrees of maturity in the mode of organising the social and moral order.

The child's moral judgement changes as he grows older. Child begins with a morality of constrain in which moral judgements are based on external authority and rigid interpretation of rules and regulations, and passes finally to a morality of cooperation in which judgements are based on social considerations and a flexible interpretation of previously inflexible rules. "All morality consists in a system of rules and the essence of all morality is to be sought in the respect which an individual acquires for these rules." Thus the development of moral judgement can be looked at in terms of a changing attitude to rules. Piaget frequently makes it perfectly clear that moral judgements are only really morally valid when they are made from a position of moral independence. At the stage of equality both logical and legal processes are involved in the judgements made.

The morally mature person has certain abilities to make right moral judgements –

i) ***Ability to collect data** (in a situation* involving *morality)*: Moral issues and moral conflicts are a common experience in the daily life of every person. Right decision making in such situations demands an ability to collect all the relevant facts of the situation (data), analyse them, think of the alternative/possible courses of action so as to facilitate the agent to take the right decision. This also involves (moral) thinking and is very similar to the scientific method of solving problems. This principle demands a few virtues such as, reasoning, endurance, patience, etc. However it is an ability demanding much more than is covered by these virtues.

ii) ***Ability to take a decision***: One may collect all the facts relevant to a situation. Yet he may not know how to proceed further. Moral education must train the agent to be able to take the right decision. Otherwise he will be a man of undecision like Hamlet. This principle contains in it a few virtues like justice, temperance, wisdom, etc.

iii) ***Will to act on the decision:*** Even after taking a decision one may fail to act under some pretext or the other for want of sufficient courage, or fear of some kind anticipated by him. In other words he may lack the determination or the will to act. Moral education must train the agent in this quality also. This principle contains in it several virtues such as courage, duty, responsibility, etc.

iv) ***To postpone gratification of desire:*** This involves the ability to endure appetite or other kind of want. An example very appropriate, for this trait is that of Sir Phillip Sydney who, himself lying wounded and thirsty in the battlefield, made over the water brought for him to an ordinary soldier of his, who was on the verge of death, saying 'Thy need is greater than mine'. In daily life every individual will come across opportunities to postpone satisfying his wants/needs with a view to oblige a friend or a relative or even a stranger.

v) ***To treat other human beings with dignity:*** This is almost similar to the first moral principle advocated by J. Wilson. This quality is named 'Moral Personalism' by William Kay.' In his opinion, the degree to which an individual is capable of treating others as persons is moral personalism and this quality in a person is directly related to the extent to which he, himself, as a child, was treated as a person.

vi) To be flexible in making moral judgements: This means that in taking moral decisions one should not follow the letter of the law but its spirit. Besides one should not treat a moral law as a legal code but be flexible, whenever such flexibility is deserved by the agent for some valid reasons. In particular wherever there is need for compassion or mercy, pardon or excuse moral decisions should be seasoned with the appropriate consideration. Portia requesting Shylock 'to season justice with mercy' is an apt example for this. The moral judge should not behave like an over-liberal parent/teacher who would not care to guide the child in matters of behaviour and morality, nor like a rigid authoritarian parent/teacher who is always dogmatic. On the other hand he is rational, yet sympathetic.

vii) To be creative and dynamic in moral decisions: Kay William (1970) is of the opinion that a moral person must be active, positive and dynamic in his behaviour so that his decisions will tend to be morally creative at least on some occasions. The moral creativity desired here, says Kay William, is not that of a dictator or of a cruel monarch but that of a person who looks on others, with love and sympathy and decides issues rationally. We may here illustrate moral creativity by an example. "If a homicidal maniac were to inquire how he would reach his victim, few would hesitate to deceive him," says Mackenzie. But when the question how to resolve this conflict was posed to Gandhiji, he replied, it is said, that he would tell the homicidal maniac that he knew where the victim was hiding, but would not disclose the place to him (maniac), come what may. How creative is this decision and true to the Gandhian principles of truth and non-violence.

The problem of inculcating the ability among children to judge morally is infested with many problems. Even though the individual's innate intelligence may be quite substantial, whether he is helped to use it for the purpose of development of moral judgement and ethical and social values is another question. The student when he uses his intelligence for other purposes, then his intelligence becomes a pervert intelligence. An immoral person is not intelligent but his intelligence is being used for other dubious purposes.

Religion provides a common ground for development of moral sense. But the system of education must take a positive action in properly directing the development of moral values among children for which it has to assess the judgement of students in respect of their own moral perception. It is this aspect of the need to identify and clarify the level and extent of moral judgement among children, that must get sustained attention and action of the educators.

PARENTAL BEHAVIOUR

Parents play an influential role in their children's moral development as home is the first school for the child where the children spend maximum time with their parents. This is revealed by the studies conducted by Parikh (1968); Walker and Taylor (1972); Garg (1983); Wallac, Whiting and Whiting, Kluchonhn (1986) and Boas (1987). Symonds (1939), Radke (1946) and Orlansky (1949) reviewed the early studies in the field of Parent-child relationship. Symonds was of the opinion that the quality of Parent-child relationship is of crucial importance in the personality development of the child. Since the most extensive and intensive social interaction of the child during crucial developmental stages occurs within the family and specially with the mother, the mother-child relationship would be of major importance in the personality development.

Parents sometimes follow only tradition in bringing up children. If the parents are very strict, children suffer from a sense of fear of punishment. The child's only concern will be how to avoid punishment. This may ultimately lead him to disobey authority, if he could go undeterred. Such treatment will not help the development of moral judgement because moral development of the child also depends on his emotional faculty. Norman J. Bull (1963) calls this type as 'Crude Heteronomy' and the discipline caused by it as physical discipline. In such homes children suffer from want of love and security and their parents do not show sufficient sympathy for any wrong inadvertently committed by the former.

On the other hand, in homes where the parents are wise and either too strict nor too liberal, the children enjoy suitable environment for their moral development. The parents advice their children regarding the right type of moral behaviour and give convincing reasons as to how it is right. They also bring home to children the possible adverse effect such as social disapproval or personal danger to them resulting from their wrong behaviour. This type of rational heteronomy helps children to develop guilt feelings for the wrong committed by them and thus sows the seed of conscience in them. Wise parents entrust children with responsibilities suited to their age capacity and thus encourage in them a feeling of self confidence. Children of such homes always enjoy the love and security of their parents. If by chance these children are found to do any morally wrong act, the parents blame themselves for their neglect. They do not blame the children or punish them. Norman J. Bull calls such discipline as psychological discipline.

Studies by McCord, Walters, Abramson Bandura (1963), Andry (1957), indicate that over aggressive and anti social behaviour is associated with parental rejection, physical punishments or threat of punishment in consistent to rules and treatment particular permissiveness to low level of parental supervision, parental interaction with the child's achievement in life and family discard. Glueck and Glueck (1950) found that less use of physical punishment in childhood and the more reasoning results in children and adolescents lesser involvement in delinquent behaviour.

The family's role is crucial. Parents are the primary moral educators of their children and they have much more time on task than a teacher. But families need schools to help them. Parents need additional education to assist their being authoritative as they raise their families. Parents should require obedience, but provide clear reasons for their expectations. Permissive parents (those who are reluctant to set rules and confront transgressions) and authoritarian parents (those who set rules but give no reasons) are not as effective as authoritative parents. Parents need to know their children's friends, and they need additional help to be taught to deal with problems that concern their children. Because nothing short of parental revolt will stop what is happening. If parents win, they would have successfully stopped an insidious plan for the hearts and minds of their children. If they lose they will be plunged into a nightmare of plummeting test scores. Privacy invasive tests politically correct, culturally diverse curriculum and children who will not be able to read or write.

It is the responsibility of the parents to mould and beautify the child, prepare him to face the world of tomorrow and to lead and guide the world of the future. It is a tremendous responsibility. Once we realize it, we will be handling the children much more intelligently by giving enough respect, reverence, true love and affection to our children.

The investigator was thus justified in including parental behaviour as one of the important variables influencing the moral development of children. It is the duty of the parents to inculcate the idea of right and wrong in the young minds. Therefore parental behaviour has been considered as one of the independent variables. In the present study the impact of mother's behaviour on adolescent children has been studied.

CHILD REARING PRACTICES

When one considers the role of parents in a child's life, there are a few facts and a few elementary principles that should be kept in mind. Each child from early infancy has his/her individual temperamental and behavioural style. Research studies reveal that parental behaviour has a remarkable effect on children (Osofsky, 1971; Yarrow, Waxler and Scott, 1971; Ashton, 1973).

In an interesting investigation of relationships between infants and mothers behaviour. Beckwith (1971, 1972) reports that the amount of physical and verbal contact with the baby and amount of experience with people other than the mother were factors of importance. Infants who had more physical and verbal contact with the mother and more experience with other people initiated more interactions with and responded more to both mother and a stranger. The more suppressive and critical the mother, the less responsive the baby was in social play, that is the child becomes less expressive and less responsive.

The role of a parent obviously involves more than a succession of separate acts. Shirley (1941) has maintained that the attitudes and personality of the mother determine the manner in which the mother administers each phase of child care. From a study of 25 mothers Behrens (1954) concluded that a child's upbringing is influenced more by quality of mothers – character structure and its effect on the total 'mother-child interactions' than by scientific child rearing practices and techniques.

It is true that like many lower animals, the infants comes helpless into the world. In his early years of life the infant is completely dependent on parents for his existence, his early mode of behaviour and development of several cognitive as well as non-cognitive abilities. If child receive neglected or harshly treatment form his parent then he started to learn aggressive acts which ultimately affect his abilities, capacities and other features of development. Symond (1949) rightly pointed that regarding child-rearing practices, "If he enjoys normal vigour and has a well functioning of glandular and nervous system, the neglected or frustrated child may depend upon the various forms of offences and aggression. Those who parents failed to guide their children into analysing their individual potential weakness, talents and interests destroy the child's personality. If they have high expectations and use a strict disciplinary pattern, they created various mal-adjustment problems in their children, which may block the development of their physical as well as mental capacities or abilities." Finding showed that dependency as either an acquired motives or an operant activity beginning in infants striving for physical gratification from parents (Beller, 1955, 1959; Healther, 1955; Houstakos, Sigel and Scholock, 1956 and Sears, 1963). Kall and Aldone (1960) studied the trends in child care over three generations and found that child rearing values of children have changed due to change of child-rearing practices.

A great deal has been written to advise parents regarding the countless practical details and decision of everyday child care. Such advice may be helpful, but it may be rather futile. No prescription for the child rearing can be equally appropriate for all children in view of their great individual differences. Notions about the right way to bring up children change with time, so that what is right in one generation may be wrong in the next (Wolfenstein, 1953).

Considering the cultural diversity of the country and the varying rural-urban proportion, meaningful generalizations on child-rearing practices in India are not permissible. The rural areas present their traditions of joint family-living and diffusion of child care responsibility.

When the child is born, the responsibility of its rearing rests with elders who are around the child most of the time. The mother feeds the child when it is hungry. Contact with the father is rare. The child learns to grow in the company of grand parents and inculcates their values, ways and manners, etc. The urban setting mostly comprises small families, so the parents themselves have to look after their children with the result that the child has direct contact with its parents.

It is empirically and generally believed that children acquire their fundamental values and attitudes from their parents; especially due to the child-rearing practices (Bales, 1955; Sears, 1957; Mead, 1955). The best nurture for a child is provided – (i) in home (ii) primarily with mother's affection, (iii) in an interact family consisting of an unseparated father and mother, (iv) providing continuity in the child's upbringing and (v) in an atmosphere of loving acceptance. The inclusion of child rearing practices as a independent variable is justified in the light of the above discussion.

EMOTIONAL MATURITY

The development of emotions begins at birth and continues through adolescence. The very young child's emotional experience constitutes general all over patterns of response. Gradually the various emotional reactions become localized and definitive. By the time an individual has attained emotional maturity characteristics patterns of emotional behaviour have become habituated. Emotional maturity is always relative. A five year old has emotional maturity if he is capable of the emotional behaviour we judge fitting for a five year old. Emotional maturity, however, develops throughout life. The child becomes more emotionally mature as the parent permits him to accept responsibilities and to become independent and self-sufficient.

Jersild (1967) presents one of the most comprehensive lists of the stages involved in the child's moving towards maturity in the emotional area:

1) A change from being a creature who at first receives much, gives little, to one who is capable of giving as well as receiving, and capable of learning to get employment from giving.
2) Development of capacity to identify oneself with a larger social group, and the ability to participate emotionally in the fortunes of the larger group.
3) Development from the status of being the child of the family to the status, ultimately, of being able to have children of one's own and along with this development, a capacity to exercise the feelings and attitudes involved in being a parent psychologically, whether or not one is a parent biologically.
4) An emotionally mature individual has an increased capacity for bearing the inevitable suffering and pains connected with life and growth without feeling abused.
5) An increased capacity for sympathy and compassion as one assimilates the meaning for self and other jobs and vicissitudes of life. Emotional maturity is not a state in which all problems are solved, but, instead in a continual process of clarification and evaluation, an attempt to integrate feeling, thinking and behaviour.

Emotions may well be the most important factor in the moral behaviour of most people. Certainly, it would be difficult to imagine a moral dilemma or an occasion requiring a moral choice in which the emotions were not involved in some way or the other. There is some evidence to suggest that moral character is much more a result of deep emotional forces operating during the child's formative years than of any attempts that are made at offering him rational guidance, and the work of psychologists in general on moral behaviour and moral thinking reveals quite clearly the importance of feeling in this area of human experience.

Moral Judgements are rarely made without emotional involvement of some kind. The moral judgement is usually accompanied by objectives describing human states and verbs describing human behaviour. The child's moral judgement changes as he grows older. Child begins with a morality of constraint in which moral judgements are based on external authority and right interpretation of rules and regulations, and focuses finally to a morality of cooperation in which judgements are based on social considerations and a flexible interpretation of previously inflexible rules.

Moral judgement also involves, other factors such as religion, intelligence, values and SES and not least the emotional which we find to be heavily tune to moral concepts of children and so to colour their moral judgement. Moral judgements thus becomes a short hand term for the various aspects of the total personality expressed in its encounter with other persons.

In spite of this, however, the tendency has been for this aspect of human life and experience to be largely ignored by both philosophers and educatonists, some because they have deplored the very existence of man's emotional life and have regarded it as an obstacle to be overcome rather than as a feature to be given full weight in its own right in any consideration of moral behaviour.

There is a growing realisation on the part of the schools that they must play a more active role in developing programs which stimulate positive mental health. The development of emotionally mature behaviour is a goal of education. In arranging the total school programme, school administrators must take into consideration the significance of the basic emotional needs. There is also an increased need for early recognition and identification of emotional disturbances. Each child needs to feel a sense of accomplishment and to be interested in some aspect of the school programme.

The teacher is in continual interaction with the student. Teachers, too, need to understand when behaviour is normal and when it is symptom of something wrong. The cause for the emotional deviation should be sought, and when behaviour is excessively immature, the services of a skilled guidance person should be obtained. Whether or not teachers realise it, the emotional stability of children is to a considerable extent influenced by teacher behaviour. The young child is sensitive to the teachers' attitude on a variety of school issues. A smile or a few words of sincere praise and encouragement may provide the child with the feeling of adequacy which he needs. On the other hand, the teacher's ridicule and criticism may lead to a sense of inferiority or anxiety. When a child cannot find satisfaction, through active constructive behaviour he frequently tries to solve his problem through utilisation of the defence mechanism. Teachers, therefore, should work to develop constructive means of seeing that each child's basic needs are met in the classroom.

PERSONALITY TRAITS

A system of moral and ethical code is indispensable to group living. The social structure of our society is quite complex and since the welfare of all depends upon the cooperation of all, the need for common moral principles becomes more imperative. No society can survive without a moral order. Our society is passing through the process of modernisation, providing new economic and social opportunities to even weaker sections creating thereby a transformation of character. We are at the cross roads and wondering whether it is better to welcome scientific technology, industrialisation and urbanisation at the cost of our morals. Modernisation does not mean a refusal to recognise the importance of moral and spiritual values and self-discipline.

Modernisation, if it is to be a living force, must derive its strength from the spirit. Among other things it aims at creating an economy of plenty, which will offer to every individual a large way of life and a wider variety of choices. The expanding knowledge and growing power which modernisation places at the disposal of modern society must, therefore, be combined with the strengthening and deepening of the sense of social responsibility and appreciation of moral and spiritual values, while a combination of ignorance with goodness may be futile, that of knowledge with lack of essential values may be dangerous. To reconcile modernisation and the moral values, it behooves upon our educationists to provide opportunities for the inculcation of moral attitudes and for the formation of the character of our children, adolescents and adults. If our education could foster this attitude in children along with vast store of knowledge and wisdom, it will lead the nation to the right direction.

Research studies like Symonds (1938), Levy (1942), Baldwia (1945), Kanner (1948), Shoben (1949), Sears (1957), Hess (1970), Maccoby, et al. (1975), Blehar and Others (1977), Harrington, *et al.* (1978), Rohner (1980-81), Faizunnisa (1965, 1967), Iffat Unnisa (1965), Nalini Devi (1967), Alit Rama (1967), Warty (1970), Pariera and Tirtha (1972), Patel (1965), Fictor (1975), Sidhana and Sinha (1975), Choudhari (1975), Hussain (1970), Bhogle (1978-79), Saraswati (1979), Singh (1981), Chauhan and Tiwari (1981) have pointed out the effects of different maternal attitudes on the personality development of the child. The home and the neighbourhood play a predominant role in the development of the moral character of the child. These researches show that dishonest and delinquent behaviour tend to grow out of bad family relations, low level neighbourhood and inferior personal achievement. The children who were dishonest had no adequate home training or motivational environment for honesty in their neighbourhood. Such children, motivated by their frustrations and in a bid to achieve status and satisfaction adopted dishonest behaviour. Further the study by Mirchandani (1970), on the personality profiles of delinquent and non-delinquent girls revealed that the institutionalised developed children received the most unfavourable familial attitude.

Thus the study of the moral and ethical development of children suggests, first, that importance of early, continuous and consistent training in moral development in home and schools is essentially necessary for proper development of the character of the individual; second, that moral attitudes are learnt in the same way as some other type of behaviour; third, that family and school may help the child a lot to generalise his experiences and to develop ethical principles and a well balanced personality.

SOCIO-ECONOMIC STATUS

Factors such as socio-economic status, ordinal position, sex, ethnicity, intelligence, religious background and, above all, familial discipline are increasingly recognised to be key factors in moral development.

Piaget, deriving his whole thesis from testing children from 'the poorer parts of Geneva', was aware that different results would certainly have derived from children of a different social stratum, if only in terms of age differences. Within two years of the publication of his findings, a follow-up research in London, testing children from a similar working-class background with a matching control group from cultured and well-to-do homes, found serious defects in Piaget's conclusions (Harrower, 1934). While similar results were derived from working class children, the results from the subjects of high socio-economic class were very different both in quality and quantity, with markedly maturer responses from the younger subjects, and no evidence of Piaget's age evolution. The home background was patently a powerfully influential factor. Further studies confirmed this conclusion. Moral realism declined earlier in children from higher status homes; they showed far less tendency to think of moral principles as immutable and external.

Cross-cultural studies – for example, of white American, Chinese-American, American-Indian and African children – provided further evidence of both social class and ethnic differences, and of interesting subtleties. Thus the higher judgements of Chinese-American children, as compared with white American, could be attributed to the moralising influence of a Confucian background. American-Indian children, attending a white school, while fluid in their attitudes to white games, such as baseball, regarding the rules of their tribal games as sacrosanct and unchangeable.

Sociology makes us increasingly aware of the influence of social classes, each sub-grouping having its characteristic mores. Morality is a social construct, and therefore conscience has a social genesis, the influence of the socio-economic background is manifestly powerful. Children from higher-status homes have an interwoven complex of advantages over those from a poor background. Their greater security, both economically and emotionally, gives them freedom from temptations that beset less fortunate children. It is the child from a low-status background who is tempted to steal what he needs, to be punitive in his judgements, to seek to compensate by cheating for the mental disadvantages he so often suffers.

SEX DIFFERENCES

Piaget, overwhelmingly concerned with the cognitive element in moral judgement, characteristically took boys for his subjects because of their moral developed legal sense. Many subsequent studies did likewise. In the following 25 years, only three took possible sex differences into account. Such evidence as has been found has suggested trends rather than statistically significant differences between the sexes. The question remained open.

By testing an equal number of boys and girls at every age investigators were able to observe the sex factor in every area, and in both written and verbal tests. They observed an immense sex difference. Girls were found to be in advance of boys in their moral judgements in every area examined. Four factors must be taken into account: the earlier maturation of girls; the possibility of an earlier, parallel development in intelligence; the greater facility of girls to verbalise, so that their subtlety of expression might appear to give added quality to their responses; and what some previous research has regarded as the more strict judgements of girls. The fact remains, however, that after detailed analysis of the possible relevance of their factors, the sex difference remained clear-cut.

Girls have the innate advantages, revealed in various moral situations, of greater initial sympathy, of stronger feeling for others, and therefore of far more profound sensitivity to personal relationships and social attitudes. They soar ahead of boys in their insights and attitudes and not least in those areas, such as lying, which pierce to the heat of personal relationships. Boys progress stolidly, far less spectacularly; they excel girls only in their residual anomy, and in their greater dependence upon heteronomy. Girls show far stronger socionomy, and much earlier progress towards autonomy. Only at 17 years of age have boys plodded to within striking distance of girls in their moral judgements. But even then the development as such is broadly completed, the gap remains.

Boys cxcel in the concrete situation, girls in the subleties, both good and bad, of personal relationships. Girls are mainly concerned with the psychological and personal, boys with the physical; girls with being, boys with doing. Girls expound subtle niceties of personal relationships of which boys are blissfully unaware. Boys have temptations – for example, stealing, cruelty to animals, damage to property, self-indulgence – that leave girls serenely untroubled. It is girls who are profoundly concerned with lying, deceit, unkindness, selfishness.

The stronger innate sympathy of girls develops into an earlier sense of reciprocity, and reciprocity, in turn, into greater economy. While socionomy remains strong in girls, even in maturity, they achieve autonomy earlier than boys, strikingly so in terms of truth-telling. Indeed, so strong is the advance of girls to autonomy by 13 years that they show small development thereafter. It is not until 17 years the boys achieve a similar level of autonomy, in this situation. It was only in the stark issue of life and death that boys kept anything like in step with girls in their judgements. For the rest, girls are early developers, boys are late developers. But it is not simply in terms of development that the sex difference is patent. It is there, in one form or another, from 7 years to 17 years, above all in relationships between persons. If concern for others is the heart of all morality, as indeed it must be, the female is inherently more truly moral than the male.

TYPE OF MANAGEMENT

Though it is clear to many that type of management influences the level of moral judgement in students, Rao and Mehta (1979), Du Freez (1977), Gorman (1979) concluded that the type of management has influence over the moral judgement of the students. This variable is yet to achieve adequate research attention. The relative neglect of the variable as a research area is because of the lack of realisation on the part of researchers about its plausible impact in this regard.

3.4. HYPOTHESES

The following null hypotheses have been formulated for empirical validation.

<u>Correlation Analysis</u>

Major Hypothesis

1. There is no significant relationship between different dimensions of moral judgement of students and their parental behaviour.

2. There is no significant relationship between different dimensions of moral judgement of students and their Father Oriented Child Rearing Practices.
3. There is no significant relationship between different dimensions of moral judgement of students and their Mother Oriented Child Rearing Practices.
4. There is no significant relationship between different dimensions of moral judgement of students and their Emotional Maturity.
5. There is no significant relationship between different dimensions of moral judgement of students and their Personality Traits (Extroversion).
6. There is no significant relationship between different dimensions of moral judgement of students and their Personality Traits (Introversion).
7. There is no significant relationship between different dimensions of moral judgement of students and their Personality Traits (Ambiversion).
8. There is no significant difference in the different dimensions of Moral Judgement of students as per differences in their Parental Behaviour.
9. There is no significant difference in the different dimensions of Moral Judgement of students as per differences in their Father oriented Child Rearing Practices.
10. There is no significant difference in the different dimensions of Moral Judgement of students as per differences in their Mother oriented Child Rearing Practices.
11. There is no significant difference in the different dimensions of Moral Judgement of students as per differences in their Self Knowledge Component of Emotional Maturity.

12. There is no significant difference in the different dimensions of Moral Judgement of students as per differences in their Self Confidence Component of Emotional Maturity.
13. There is no significant difference in the different dimensions of Moral Judgement of students as per differences in their Acceptance of Reality Component of Emotional Maturity.
14. There is no significant difference in the different dimensions of Moral Judgement of students as per differences in their Self Control Component of Emotional Maturity.
15. There is no significant difference in the different dimensions of Moral Judgement of students as per differences in their Social Adjustment Component of Emotional Maturity.
16. There is no significant difference in the different dimensions of Moral Judgement of students as per differences in their Consistency Component of Emotional Maturity.
17. There is no significant difference in the different dimensions of Moral Judgement of students as per differences in their total Emotional Maturity.
18. There is no significant difference in the different dimensions of Moral Judgement of students as per differences in their personality traits (Extroverts, Introverts and Ambiverts).
19. There is no significant difference in the different dimensions of Moral Judgement of students as per differences in their parents' socio-economic status.
20. There is no significant difference in the different dimensions of Moral Judgement of students as per differences in their sex.

21. There is no significant difference in the different dimensions of Moral Judgement of students as per differences in the type of management in which they are studying.
22. There is no significant main and interaction effect of sex and type of management on the Moral Judgement of students.
23. There is no significant main and interaction effect of sex and parental behaviour on the Moral Judgement of students.
24. There is no significant main and interaction effect of sex and Father oriented Child Rearing Practices on the Moral Judgement of students.
25. There is no significant main and interaction effect of sex and Mother oriented Child Rearing Practices on the Moral Judgement of students.
26. There is no significant main and interaction effect of sex and Emotional Maturity on the Moral Judgement of students.
27. There is no significant main and interaction effect of sex and Personality Traits on the Moral Judgement of students.
28. There is no significant main and interaction effect of sex and socio-economic status on the Moral Judgement of students.
29. There is no significant main and interaction effect of type of management and parental behaviour on the Moral Judgement of students.
30. There is no significant main and interaction effect of type of management and Father oriented Child Rearing Practices on the Moral Judgement of students.
31. There is no significant main and interaction effect of type of management and Mother oriented Child Rearing Practices on the Moral Judgement of students.

32. There is no significant main and interaction effect of type of management and Emotional Maturity on the Moral Judgement of students.
33. There is no significant main and interaction effect of type of management and Personality Traits on the Moral Judgement of students.
34. There is no significant main and interaction effect of type of management and socio-economic status on the Moral Judgement of students.
35. There is no significant main and interaction effect of parental behaviour and Father oriented Child Rearing Practices on the Moral Judgement of students.
36. There is no significant main and interaction effect of parental behaviour and Mother oriented Child Rearing Practices on the Moral Judgement of students.
37. There is no significant main and interaction effect of parental behaviour and Emotional Maturity on the Moral Judgement of students.
38. There is no significant main and interaction effect of parental behaviour and Personality Traits on the Moral Judgement of students.
39. There is no significant main and interaction effect of parental behaviour and socio-economic status on the Moral Judgement of students.
40. There is no significant main and interaction effect of Father oriented Child Rearing Practices and Mother oriented Child Rearing Practices on the Moral Judgement of students.
41. There is no significant main and interaction effect of Father oriented Child Rearing Practices and Emotional Maturity on the Moral Judgement of students.
42. There is no significant main and interaction effect of Father oriented Child Rearing Practices and Personality Traits on the Moral Judgement of students.

43. There is no significant main and interaction effect of Father oriented Child Rearing Practices and socio-economic status on the Moral Judgement of students.
44. There is no significant main and interaction effect of Mother oriented Child Rearing Practices and Emotional Maturity on the Moral Judgement of students.
45. There is no significant main and interaction effect of Mother oriented Child Rearing Practices and Personality Traits on the Moral Judgement of students.
46. There is no significant main and interaction effect of Mother oriented Child Rearing Practices and socio-economic status on the Moral Judgement of students.
47. There is no significant main and interaction effect of Emotional Maturity and Personality Traits on the Moral Judgement of students.
48. There is no significant main and interaction effect of Emotional Maturity and socio-economic status on the Moral Judgement of students.
49. There is no significant main and interaction effect of Personality Traits and socio-economic status on the Moral Judgement of students.

3.5. SAMPLING PROCEDURE

Population of the Study:

All the students of the 10th standard in all the schools belonging to Government, aided and unaided categories of Bangalore North and South district formed the population of the study. There were 85, 237 and 602 Government, aided and unaided secondary schools respectively in Bangalore North and South districts at the time of data collection.

Since the researcher wanted to draw the sample from relatively larger area, included all the 10th standard students of secondary schools of Bangalore North and South for her population. The details of population of school are given in the following table.

Table 3.1: Population of school in Bangalore City

District	Type of school			Total
	Govern ment	Aide d	Unaide d	
Bangalore North District	40	111	258	409
Bangalore South District	45	126	344	515
TOTAL	85	237	602	924

Sampling Design

The sample was drawn following a two-stage stratified random sampling technique. At the first stage a total of 20 schools have been drawn from the total of 924 schools. At this stage simple random sampling was resorted to. In total, 4 government, 8 private aided and 8 private unaided schools were selected. At the second stage, 250 male and 250 female students were selected from the 20 schools. The representation of male and female students in the three types of management is as follows:

There were 86 boys and 83 girls from government schools, 82 boys and 79 girls from private aided schools and 82 boys and 88 girls from private unaided schools respectively.

Table 3.2

Showing Number of Students selected from three different types of schools of Bangalore City

Gender	Type of School			Total
	Government	Aided	Unaided	
Boys	86	82	82	250
Girls	83	79	88	250
Total	169	161	170	500

3.6. TOOLS OF THE STUDY

Sl. No.	Name of the Tool	Author
1.	Moral Judgement Scale	B.G. Sudha & B.S. Sathyanarayana
2.	Children's Report of Parental Behaviour Inventory	Dr. Uma Saxena & Dr. N.K. Saxena
3.	Child Rearing Practices Test	Roma Pal and Karim
4.	Emotional Maturity Scale	Dr. Tara Sabapathy
5.	Introversion and Extroversion Inventory	Ramanatha Kundu
6.	Socio-economic Scale	Kuppuswamy

MORAL JUDGEMENT SCALE

A scale developed by Dr. B.G. Sudha and B.S. Sathyanarayana was used to measure the moral judgement of the 10th standard students in the present study. It is a self-reporting scale, the items of which are situational. The scale consists of 30 items. The scale measures the following five dimensions of moral judgement.

a) Honesty (measured by items 1, 6, 11, 16, 21, 26)
b) Truthfulness (measured by items 2, 7, 12, 17, 22, 27)
c) Non-violence (measured by items 3, 8, 13, 18, 23, 28)
d) Obedience (measured by items 4, 9, 14, 19, 24, 29)
e) Justice (measured by items 5, 10, 15, 20, 25, 30)

Scoring Procedure

Moral judgement scale is a three-point scale. Items of the scale are in the form of statements, demanding responses from the 3 options provided. The moral judgement scale was scored by giving 1, 2 and 3 scores for the 1st, 2nd and 3rd alternatives depending on the extent of increase in judgement.

Reliability of the Scale

A test score is said to be reliable when the scores are stable and trustworthy. Stability and trustworthiness depend upon the degree to which the score is an index of the true ability or is free of chance error. Two types or reliabilities have been established.

Test-Retest Reliability

Co-efficients computed by this method are frequently called co-efficient of stability. The test was given and repeated on a group of 120 secondary school students and the correlation was computed between the first and second sets of scores by using Pearson Product Moment Correlation. The obtained 'r' was found to be 0.70 with time gap of one month between the two administrations.

Split-Half Method

The split-half method is employed when it is not feasible to construct parallel forms of the test nor advisable to repeat the test itself. This is because, if the test is repeated or given in its alternate form, the response of the subject may change while taking the test the second time.

The split-half method is considered to be the best method for establishing reliability. Its main advantage is that the main data for computing reliability is obtained in one occasion, so that variations brought about by differences between the two testing situations are eliminated.

To establish the reliability of the tool, the split half method was employed. The scores obtained from the try out group, on the test, were divided into two equivalent 'tests' and the correlation was found for these half-tests. From the reliability of the half-test the self-correlation of the whole test was estimated by the Spearman-Brown Prophecy formula.

The procedure adopted is two sets of scores were formed by taking the alternate items in the test. The first set of scores represents performance on the odd numbered items – 1, 3, 5, 7, 9, etc. and the second set of scores represents performance on the even numbered items – 2, 4, 6, 8, 10, etc. Then, to find out the coefficient of correlation between the odd numbered and even numbered items for each student, Pearson Product Moment Correlation was used. The obtained correlation value was found to be 0.60.

From the self-correlation of the half tests, the reliability co-efficient of the whole test was established using the Spearman Brown Prophecy formula, the correlation value obtained for the whole test was 0.75.

Sl. No.	Reliability	Coefficient Correlation	Index of Reliability √r
1.	**Split-half**	0.75	0.86
2.	Test-retests (one month)	0.70	0.83

Validity of the Scale

The validity of a test depends upon the fidelity with which it measures, what it purports to measure. A test is valid when the performance which it measures corresponds to the same performance as otherwise independently defined. Validity is a relative term, and a test can be valid for a particular purpose or in a particular situation and, not in all situations. To establish the validity of the tool constructed, different types of validity measures are adopted. They are:

(i) **Content Validity:** The choice of an item depends in the first instance upon the judgement of competent persons as to its suitability for the purpose of the test. This establishes the content validity. Content validity is a non-statistical type of validity, its strength depends on the rigorous theoretical exercise employed in its application. Therefore the tool was content validated by experts in the specialised field.

(ii) **Cross Validity:** The scale is said to possess the cross validity since the sample selected for try-out of the statement was not included in the establishment of reliability and validity of the scale. This avoids the chance error of increasing the reliability co-efficient.

(iii) **Item Validity:** This was established by selecting the items which had significant 'r' values on item total correlation. All the 30 items were significant at 0.01 level.

CHILDREN'S REPORT OF PARENTAL BEHAVIOUR INVENTORY

An inventory originally developed by Dr. Uma Saxena and Dr. N.K.Saxena in Hindi was first translated by language experts from the Department of Hindi, Bangalore University, Bangalore and later standardised by the investigator was used to measure the Children's report of the Parental Behaviour in the present study.

The following table gives the scale-wise locations of the items of all the 18 areas of the children's report of Parental Behaviour Inventory.

CRPBI Scales	Item Location
1. Acceptance	1, 14, 43, 50, 59, 76, 83, 96.
2. Child-centeredness	15, 31, 60, 84, 97.
3. Possessiveness	36, 51, 65, 89, 103.
4. Rejection	2, 23, 44, 52, 61, 71, 85, 104.
5. Control	3, 16, 32, 72, 98.
6. Enforcement	9, 24, 37, 77, 105.
7. Positive Involvement	17, 38, 53, 66, 86, 90, 99, 106.
8. Intrusiveness	4, 18, 33, 45, 73.
9. Control Through Guilt	10, 39, 67, 78, 91.
10. Hostile Control	11, 25, 34, 54, 74, 79, 92, 100.
11. Inconsistent Discipline	5, 19, 46, 62, 101.
12. Non-enforcement	12, 26, 55, 68, 80.
13. Acceptance of Individuation	20, 27, 35, 40, 63, 69, 87, 93.
14. Lack Discipline	6, 21, 47, 75, 102.
15. Instilling Persistent Anxiety	28, 4, 56, 81, 107.
16. Hostile Detachment	7, 13, 29, 48, 57, 70, 82, 94.
17. Withdrawal of Relations	8, 22, 49, 64, 88.
18. Extreme Autonomy	30, 42, 58, 95, 108.

From the perusal of the above table we find that 12 CRPBI scales contain 5-items each and the remaining 6 scales contain 8 items each. Each item is assigned a score of 3, 2 or 1 according to the response L, SL or NL respectively. To calculate scale scores, add scores (3, 2 or 1) of all the statement of each scale. Divide the total score of each scale by 5 in case of 5-item scales and by 8 in case of 3-item scales. Multiply this by 10.

Reliability

The test-retest reliability was computed (N = 200) and the *r* was found to be .77. Split-half reliability (N = 200) was found to be .81.

Validity

The original tool was in Hindi and it was therefore necessary to translate it into the English version. The tool was given to language experts who were proficient in both languages namely Hindi and English for translation and content validation. The translated tool (English version) along with the Hindi version was administered to 120, students studying in Bangalore City. The two sets of scores obtained by 120, 10th standard students were correlated. The obtained co-efficient correlation which was 0.83 was high enough thus proving the validity of the translated version of the scale.

Uses of CRPBI

CRPBI is an instrument mainly for measuring children's attitude toward their Parental behaviour (mother form). It has already been pointed out in the introduction that children's perception of their parental behaviour is likely to influence their personality. CRPBI may be used by the researchers in the fields of Psychology, Sociology, Anthropology and Education. The tool is also useful in the sense that it can measure all or only some of the 18 areas of CRPBI.

CHILD REARING PRACTICES SCALE (for Mother and Father Forms)

A scale constructed and standardised by Dr. Roma Pal and Mrs. Shamim Karim was used to measure both child rearing practices and child rearing attitudes. It has two forms – Mother form and Father form. Father form measures five factors (1) Comfort and Encouragement, (2) Control and Supervision, (3) Acceptance and Harmony, (4) Ambivalence and (5) Does not allow independence whereas mother form has 6 factors – (1) Comfort and Encouragement, (2) Acceptance and Harmony, (3) Control Sex and Aggression: Authoritarian, (4) Punitive and Controlling, (5) Intrusiveness and (6) Maintain boundaries between child and others.

Scoring Procedure

The scoring is done on 3 point scale. A score of 1, 2 and 3 is assigned and the interpretation of the scores was done.

Reliability:

For determining the reliability of the test, the tests were administered to 300 parents (150 mothers and 150 fathers) respectively, and then split-half reliability was calculated by odd-even method which were .83 and .79 for mother and father form respectively.

Validity:

Item validity was established and only those items whose validity indices was 0.20 and above were retained for the final form of the test by the authors.

EMOTIONAL MATURITY

Emotional Maturity Scale by Tara Sabapathy was used. A scale on emotional maturity was constructed and standardised by Tara Sabapathy to assess the perception of an individual of his self knowledge, self confidence, acceptance of reality, self control, social adjustment and consistency. It is a 4 point scale consisting of 44 items.

Scoring Procedure:

The Emotional Maturity Scale containing 44 items had 22 positive and 22 negative statements. These statements were distributed unequally over the 6 components, namely self knowledge, self confidence, self concept, acceptance of reality, self control, social adjustment and consistency, with 8, 8, 6, 8, 8 and 6 items. For positive items Always, Sometimes, Rarely and Never were given a weightage of 4, 3, 2 and 1 respectively. In the case of negative items, the scoring procedure was reversed.

Reliability:

The test-retest reliability co-efficient was 0.77 and split-half reliability co-efficient of 0.69 was established.

Validity:

Criterion related validity was established for the emotional maturity scale. The most suitable external criterion was found to be the teacher's ratings on the attributes of emotional maturity. Since class teachers have ample opportunities to observe students in a variety of situations in which the behaviour in question could be manifested, it was found that teacher ratings of students on the various dimensions of emotional maturity was a good criterion for validating the scale.

The student form of the Emotional Maturity Scale items were transformed into teacher rating form, wherein the scale items could be directly observable by teachers. All the 44 items were then transformed into behavioural items taking care that the meanings of the items did not change.

The researcher sat with the teachers and entered their responses so that near accurate response would be available. A sample of 120 students equally distributed between the two sexes drawn by a stratified random sampling were rated by 8 teachers, every teacher rating 15 students. Class teachers were selected on the basis of their close contact with students every day for atleast a year. Test papers were scored and 2 sets of scores obtained by 120 students and the scores given by the eight teachers for the 120 students were correlated. The coefficient of correlation was found to be 0.72, which was fairly high. With all these the scale had met the criteria for validity fairly sufficiently and valid for the purposes of the study.

KUNDU'S INTROVERSION EXTROVERSION INVENTORY

To measure the personality type (introversion extroversion) a tool prepared by Ramanatha Kundu (1976) was used. It was developed according to Indian Sociological Pattern. The inventory contained 70 items with uneven number of responses, choices divided into 5 blocks as follows.

Number of items and responses choice in different blocks

Block	No. of Items	No. of Response Choice
A	11	4
B	17	5
C	14	3
D	14	3
E	14	2

The contents of these five blocks were divided in the following manner:

Block A: Response choices were mostly some objectives situations or activities.

Block B: Mostly introspective items.

Block C: Selection of one activity over the other but the activities are mostly of objective nature regarding oneself.

Block D: Mostly objective activities regarding oneself.

Block E: Mostly introspective forced choice items.

Scoring

The scoring key is as follows. The general order of scoring is such that high score indicated introversion, i.e., a negative response is indicative of introversion. But some of the items have been framed in such a way that negative response in these items would indicate extroversion. Classification of items from this point of view is shown in this table below.

Block	Negative answer showing Introversion. Item Serial Nos.	Positive answer showing Introversion. Item Serial Nos.
A	1, 4, 6, 10 and 11	2, 3, 5, 7, 8 and 9
B	12, 13, 15, 17, 18, 21, 22, 24, 25, 26 and 28	14, 16, 19, 20, 23 and 27
C	29, 30, 31, 32, 33, 34, 35, 37, 38, 39 and 40	36, 41 and 42
D	43, 44, 45, 46, 49, 50, 51, 52, 53, 54, 55 and 56	47 and 48
E	57, 59, 60, 61, 62, 64, 65, 68 and 69	48, 63, 66, 67 and 70

Scoring Procedure

Scoring procedure is simple and may be summarised in the following steps as the answer sheet is so designed.

1. Count the tick (3) marks in each row in each block and enter the figure under the column T against the respective row.
2. Multiply these totals (T's) in the following order

   Block A: First row total x 1
   Second row total x 2
   Third row total x 3
   Fourth row total x 4

   Block B: First row total x 1
   Second row total x 2
   Third row total x 3

	Fourth row total x 4
	Fifth row total x 5
Block C:	First row total x 1
	Second row total x 2
	Third row total x 3
Block D:	First row total x 1
	Second row total x 2
	Third row total x 3
Block E:	First row total x 1
	Second row total x 2

3. Add all the entries in the column 5 together to get the total introversion-extroversion score at a time.

Reliability

The reliability co-efficients are presented in the table below. Block reliabilities as well as total test reliability have been determined by split-half method applying Spearman-Brown formula. In addition to that reliability has also been computed by Cronbh's formula taking each block on a separate sub-test.

Reliability Co-efficient

Block	Reliability Co-efficient	
	1st half vs. 2nd half	Odds vs. Even
A	0.64	0.79
B	0.82	0.76
C	0.60	0.86
D	0.66	0.41
E	0.89	0.66
Whole Test	0.82	0.71
Whole Test by Cornbach Formula		0.73

Validity

Validity co-efficients in terms of the block total correlation are given in the table below. The inventory is also validated against introversion-extroversion score by Eysenck Personality Inventory (EPI). In EPI, the increasing order of score corresponds the KIET the order is reverse, i.e., the decreasing order of score corresponds to the degree of extroversion. Therefore co-efficient of correlation between KIET score and EPI score was expected to be negative to ensure validity of KIET. The obtained co-efficient of correlation presented in the table below was negative but it has been shown without any sign.

Validity Co-efficients

Criteria	Co-efficients of Correlation
Block A	0.41
Block B	0.77
Block C	0.42
Block D	0.55
Block E	0.49
EPI	0.47

SOCIO-ECONOMIC STATUS SCALE

The revised form of the socio-economic status scale developed by Kuppuswamy (1981) was used in the present study. This scale was used for the following reasons:

1. The scale was standardised primarily for use in socio-economic status investigations in urban parts of India.
2. It is a simple instrument which would be used without spending much time and effort.
3. Scoring procedure is very simple and clear.

The scale is on the educational level, occupational category and income of the parent/guardian. In the scale for the three categories there are weightages and accordingly the socio-economic status is to be finalised. The validity of the scale had been established (1) by validating it against an external criterion, (2) by comparing it with the scores obtained in the case of radio owners, and (3) by comparing dichotomous groups. In all the three cases there were sufficient indications of satisfactory validity indices of the scale.

3.7. ADMINISTRATION OF THE TOOLS

The Moral Judgement Scale by B.G. Sudha and B.S. Satyanarayana, the Children's Report of Parental Behaviour Inventory, adapted by the investigator, Child Rearing Practices Test by Pal and Karim, Emotional Maturity Scale by Tara Sabapathy Introversion and Extroversion Inventory by Kundu and the Socio-Economic Status Scale by Kuppuswamy was administered to the sample of 500 students from 20 different schools of Bangalore by the researcher herself. Directions were clearly given to the students as to how they should respond to each of the above tools. While administering the tools, the subjects were made to feel comfortable and were encouraged to answer freely. Each statement was read out clearly and loudly by the investigator, so that they could respond clearly and properly.

3.8. STATISTICAL ANALYSIS

Before going ahead with the analysis of data, the purposes for which different statistical techniques were used in the course of analysis of data are given so that the frame of reference of the analysis becomes clear.

	Statistical techniques	Purpose for which used
1	Zero-order correlations: (Product moment correlations)	This technique was used to find out the relationship between the five dimensions of moral judgement, namely- honesty, truthfulness, non-violence, obedience, justice and total Moral Judgement on one hand, and parental behaviour, child rearing practices, emotional maturity and personality traits on the other hand.
2	t-test Analysis	t-test was calculated to find out whether differences in the independent variables, namely- parental behaviour, child rearing practices, emotional maturity, personality traits, socio-economic status, sex and type of management would account for significant differences in five dimensions of Moral Judgement of students, namely honesty, truthfulness, non-violence, obedience and justice and total Moral Judgement.
3	Two-way ANOVA	This technique was used to find out the significance of main effects and interaction effect (2 X 2 factorial design).

The present chapter dealt with the methodology adopted by the investigator. In the next chapter the investigator presents the analysis and interpretation of the data.

CHAPTER IV

ANALYSIS AND INTERPRETATION OF DATA

In the previous chapter the methodology adopted for the present investigation has been presented. This chapter is on the analysis of data, interpretation and discussion of results.

The data collected have been analysed using Pearson's product moment co-efficient of correlation, t-test and two-way analysis of variance and the results obtained thereby have been interpreted. This has been done each independent and dependent variable wise. The purpose of this study is to find out the relationship between the dependent variable Moral Judgement of students and their Parental Behaviour, Child Rearing Practices, Emotional Maturity and Personality traits. It was also the intention of the investigator to find out whether differences in the independent variables, namely, Parental Behaviour, Child Rearing Practices, Emotional Maturity and Personality traits, Socio-Economic Status, Sex differences and Type of Management would account for significant differences in the dependent variable, Moral Judgement of students. Finally it was also the purpose of the researcher to find out the main and interaction effects of the independent variables on the dependent variable, Moral Judgement of students.

For purpose of convenience, the minor hypotheses stated for correlation and t-test analysis have been represented in single table separately for the relationship and difference between moral judgement dimensions – honesty, the truthfulness, non-violence, obedience and justice and total moral judgement on one hand, and the independent variables parental behaviour, child rearing practices, emotional maturity and personality traits on the other.

4.1 CORRELATION ANALYSIS

Major Hypothesis

1. There is no significant relationship between different dimensions of moral judgement of students and their parental behaviour.

Minor Hypotheses

1.1. There is no significant relationship between honesty dimension of moral judgement of students and their parental behaviour.

1.2. There is no significant relationship between truthfulness dimension of moral judgement of students and their parental behaviour.

1.3. There is no significant relationship between non-violence dimension of moral judgement of students and their parental behaviour.

1.4. There is no significant relationship between obedience dimension of moral judgement of students and their parental behaviour.

1.5. There is no significant relationship between justice dimension of moral judgement of students and their parental behaviour.

1.6. There is no significant relationship between total moral judgement of students and their parental behaviour.

Table 4.1

The table showing the Variables, size (N), df and Co-efficient of Correlation 'r' and its significance at 0.05 and 0.01 levels between different dimensions of Moral Judgement of Students and their Parental Behaviour.

Sl. No.	Variables Moral Judgement X Parental Behaviour Dimensions of Moral Judgement	N	df (N – 2)	'r'	Level of significance at 0.05 and 0.01 level
1.	Honesty	500	498	0.14	**
2.	Truthfulness	500	498	0.12	**
3.	Non-Violence	500	498	0.24	**
4.	Obedience	500	498	0.15	**
5.	Justice	500	498	0.17	**
6.	Total Moral Judgement	500	498	0.58	**

** Significant at 0.01 level.

From the above table it can be seen that the obtained 'r' values 0.14, 0.12, 0.24, 0.15, 0.17 and 0.58 are higher than the table value 0.088 at 0.05 level of significance and 0.115 at 0.01 level of significance. Therefore the null hypothesis was rejected at both the levels of significance. The alternate hypothesis that there is a significant and positive relationship between all dimensions of moral judgement of and their Parental Behaviour is accepted.

This coincides with the study of Garg (1983), who concludes that the development of personality and moral judgement were closely related to the type of parental disciplinary practices. Parikh (1968), In American studies the relationship of the family environmental factor to children's development of moral judgement is significantly positive where age does not count. Bhargava (1986), who says that home variables were significant predictors of moral judgement in terms of mother acceptance, socio-economic status and moral attitudes. Rao's conclusion which says that there was a significant relationship t levels of family religious practices and moral judgement scores, the latter being higher in the case of subjects coming from less rigid religious practices. Rani M. (1968) study of survey of moral development among children concludes that parents influence in the acquisition and development of moral values in children was of vital significance.

Major Hypothesis

2. There is no significant relationship between different dimensions of moral judgement of students and their Father oriented Child Rearing Practices.

Minor Hypotheses

2.1. There is no significant relationship between honesty dimension of moral judgement of students and their Father oriented Child Rearing Practices.

2.2. There is no significant relationship between truthfulness dimension of moral judgement of students and their Father oriented Child Rearing Practices.

2.3. There is no significant relationship between non-violence dimension of moral judgement of students and their Father oriented Child Rearing Practices.

2.4. There is no significant relationship between obedience dimension of moral judgement of students and their Father oriented Child Rearing Practices.

2.5. There is no significant relationship between justice dimension of moral judgement of students and their Father oriented Child Rearing Practices.

2.6. There is no significant relationship between total moral judgement of students and their Father oriented Child Rearing Practices.

Table 4.2

The table showing the Variables, size (N), df and Co-efficient of Correlation 'r' and its significance at 0.05 and 0.01 levels between different dimensions of Moral Judgement of Students and Father oriented Child Rearing Practices.

Sl. No.	Variable Moral Judgement X Father Oriented Child Rearing Practices Dimensions of Moral Judgement	N	df (N – 2)	'r'	Level of significance at 0.05 and 0.01 level
1.	Honesty	500	498	0.64	**
2.	Truthfulness	500	498	0.68	**
3.	Non-Violence	500	498	0.16	**
4.	Obedience	500	498	0.72	**
5.	Justice	500	498	0.52	**
6.	Total Moral Judgement	500	498	0.64	**

** Significant at 0.01 level.

From the above table it can be seen that the obtained 'r' values 0.64, 0.68, 0.16 0.72, 0.52 and 0.64 are higher than the table value 0.088 at 0.05 level of significance and 0.115 at 0.01 level of significance. Therefore the null hypothesis was rejected at both levels of significance. The alternate hypothesis that there is highly significant and positive relationship between all dimensions of moral judgement of and their Father oriented Child Rearing Practices is accepted.

Major Hypothesis

3. There is no significant relationship between different dimensions of moral judgement of students and their Mother oriented Child Rearing Practices.

Minor Hypotheses

3.1. There is no significant relationship between honesty dimension of moral judgement of students and their Mother oriented Child Rearing Practices.

3.2. There is no significant relationship between Truthfulness dimension of moral judgement of students and their Mother oriented Child Rearing Practices.

3.3. There is no significant relationship between non-violence dimension of moral judgement of students and their Mother oriented Child Rearing Practices.

3.4. There is no significant relationship between obedience dimension of moral judgement of students and their Mother oriented Child Rearing Practices.

3.5. There is no significant relationship between justice dimension of moral judgement of students and their Mother oriented Child Rearing Practices.

3.6. There is no significant relationship between total moral judgement of students and their Mother oriented Child Rearing Practices.

Table 4.3

The table showing the Variables, size (N), df and Co-efficient of Correlation 'r' and its significance at 0.05 and 0.01 levels between different dimensions of Moral Judgement of Students and Mother oriented Child Rearing Practices.

Sl. No.	Variable Moral Judgement X Mother Oriented Child Rearing Practices Dimensions of Moral Judgement	N	df (N – 2)	'r'	Level of significance at 0.05 and 0.01 level
1.	Honesty	500	498	0.65	**
2.	Truthfulness	500	498	0.78	**
3.	Non-Violence	500	498	0.72	**
4.	Obedience	500	498	0.73	**
5.	Justice	500	498	0.70	**
6.	Total Moral Judgement	500	498	0.54	**

** Significant at 0.01 level.

From the above table it can be seen that the obtained 'r' values 0.65, 0.78, 0.72, 0.73, 0.70 and 0.54 are much higher than the table value 0.088 at 0.05 level of significance and 0.115 at 0.01 level of significance. Therefore the null hypothesis was rejected at both 0.05 and 0.01 levels of significance. The alternate hypothesis that there is highly significant and positive relationship between all dimensions of moral judgement of and their Mother oriented Child Rearing Practices is accepted.

This finding of the present study is supported by the studies of Holstein (1972) who concludes that there is correlation between parental child rearing practices and moral development. Arunodekar, Desai and Singh (1973) concludes that mothers from higher socio-economic status were more rigid and severe in training their children than those from lower socio-economic status. Goswami, (1977) concluded that child rearing was more of mother's job than father's job.

Major Hypothesis

4. There is no significant relationship between different dimensions of moral judgement of students and their Emotional Maturity.

Minor Hypotheses

4.1. There is no significant relationship between honesty dimension of moral judgement of students and their Emotional Maturity.

4.2. There is no significant relationship between Truthfulness dimension of moral judgement of students and their Emotional Maturity.

4.3. There is no significant relationship between non-violence dimension of moral judgement of students and their Emotional Maturity.

4.4. There is no significant relationship between obedience dimension of moral judgement of students and their Emotional Maturity.

4.5. There is no significant relationship between justice dimension of moral judgement of students and their Emotional Maturity.

4.6. There is no significant relationship between total moral judgement of students and their Emotional Maturity.

Table 4.4

The table showing the Variables, size (N), df and Co-efficient of Correlation 'r' and its significance at 0.05 and 0.01 levels between different dimensions of Moral Judgement of Students and their Emotional Maturity

Sl. No.	Variable Moral Judgement X Total Emotional Maturity Dimensions of Moral Judgement	N	df (N – 2)	'r'	Level of significance at 0.05 and 0.01 level
1.	Honesty	500	498	0.73	**
2.	Truthfulness	500	498	0.51	**
3.	Non-Violence	500	498	0.59	**
4.	Obedience	500	498	0.68	**
5.	Justice	500	498	0.58	**
6.	Total Moral Judgement	500	498	0.92	**

** Significant at 0.01 level.

From the above table it can be seen that the obtained 'r' values 0.73, 0.51, 0.59, .68, 0.58 and 0.92 are higher than the table value 0.088 at 0.05 level and 0.115 at 0.01 level of significance. Therefore the null hypothesis was rejected at both 0.05 and 0.01 levels of significance. The alternate hypothesis that there is significant and positive relationship between all dimensions of moral judgement of students and their Emotional Maturity is accepted.

Major Hypothesis

5. There is no significant relationship between different dimensions of moral judgement of students and their Personality Traits (Extroversion).

Minor Hypotheses

5.1. There is no significant relationship between honesty dimension of moral judgement of students and their Personality Traits (Extroversion).

5.2. There is no significant relationship between truthfulness dimension of moral judgement of students and their Personality Traits (Extroversion).

5.3. There is no significant relationship between non-violence dimension of moral judgement of students and their Personality Traits (Extroversion).

5.4. There is no significant relationship between obedience dimension of moral judgement of students and their Personality Traits (Extroversion).

5.5. There is no significant relationship between justice dimension of moral judgement of students and their Personality Traits (Extroversion).

5.6. There is no significant relationship between total moral judgement of students and their Personality Traits (Extroversion).

Table 4.5

The table showing the Variables, size (N), df and Co-efficient of Correlation 'r' and its significance at 0.05 and 0.01 levels between different dimensions of Moral Judgement of Students and their Personality traits (Extroversion).

Sl. No.	Variables Moral Judgement X Personality Traits Dimensions of Moral Judgement	N	df (N – 2)	'r'	Level of significance at 0.05 and 0.01 level
1.	Honesty	500	498	0.63	**
2.	Truthfulness	500	498	0.68	**
3.	Non-Violence	500	498	0.61	*
4.	Obedience	500	498	0.57	**
5.	Justice	500	498	0.62	*
6.	Total Moral Judgement	500	498	0.71	**

* Significant at 0.05 level

** Significant at 0.01 level

From the above table it can be seen that the obtained 'r' values 0.63, 0.68, 0.61, 0.57, 0.62 and 0.71 are higher than the table value 0.088 at 0.05 level and 0.115 at 0.01 level of significance. Therefore the null hypothesis was rejected at 0.05 and 0.01 levels of significance. The alternate hypothesis that there is significant and positive relationship between all dimensions of moral judgement of students and their Personality Traits (Extroversion) is accepted.

Major Hypothesis

6. There is no significant relationship between different dimensions of moral judgement of students and their Personality Traits (Introversion).

Minor Hypotheses

6.1. There is no significant relationship between honesty dimension of moral judgement of students and their Personality Traits (Introversion).

6.2. There is no significant relationship between Truthfulness dimension of moral judgement of students and their Personality Traits (Introversion).

6.3. There is no significant relationship between non-violence dimension of moral judgement of students and their Personality Traits (Introversion).

6.4. There is no significant relationship between obedience dimension of moral judgement of students and their Personality Traits (Introversion).

6.5. There is no significant relationship between justice dimension of moral judgement of students and their Personality Traits (Introversion).

6.6. There is no significant relationship between total moral judgement of students and their Personality Traits (Introversion).

Table 4.6

The table showing the Variables, size (N), df and Co-efficient of Correlation 'r' and its significance at 0.05 and 0.01 levels between different dimensions of Moral Judgement of Students and their Personality traits (Introversion).

Sl. No.	Variables Moral Judgement X Personality traits Dimensions of Moral Judgement	N	df (N – 2)	'r'	Level of significance at 0.05 and 0.01 level
1.	Honesty	500	498	0.52	**
2.	Truthfulness	500	498	0.64	**
3.	Non-Violence	500	498	0.59	**
4.	Obedience	500	498	0.56	**
5.	Justice	500	498	0.67	**
6.	Total Moral Judgement	500	498	0.73	**

* Significant at 0.05 level ** Significant at 0.01 level

From the above table it can be seen that the obtained 'r' values 0.52, 0.64, 0.59, 0.56, 0.67 and 0.73 are higher than the table value 0.088 at 0.05 level and 0.115 at 0.01 level of significance. Therefore the null hypothesis was rejected at both levels of significance. The alternate hypothesis that there is significant and positive relationship between all dimensions of moral judgement of students and their Personality Traits (Introversion) is accepted.

Major Hypothesis

7. There is no significant relationship between different dimensions of moral judgement of students and their Personality Traits (Ambiversion).

Minor Hypotheses

7.1. There is no significant relationship between honesty dimension of moral judgement of students and their Personality Traits (Ambiversion).

7.2. There is no significant relationship between Truthfulness dimension of moral judgement of students and their Personality Traits (Ambiversion).

7.3. There is no significant relationship between non-violence dimension of moral judgement of students and their Personality Traits (Ambiversion).

7.4. There is no significant relationship between obedience dimension of moral judgement of students and their Personality Traits (Ambiversion).

7.5. There is no significant relationship between justice dimension of moral judgement of students and their Personality Traits (Ambiversion).

7.6. There is no significant relationship between total moral judgement of students and their Personality Traits (Ambiversion).

Table 4.7

The table showing the Variables, size (N), df and Co-efficient of Correlation 'r' and its significance at 0.05 and 0.01 levels between different dimensions of Moral Judgement of Students and their Personality traits (Ambiversion).

Sl. No.	Variables Moral Judgement X Personality traits Dimensions of Moral Judgement	N	df (N – 2)	'r'	Level of significance at 0.05 and 0.01 level
1.	Honesty	500	498	0.46	**
2.	Truthfulness	500	498	0.57	**
3.	Non-Violence	500	498	0.63	**
4.	Obedience	500	498	0.71	**
5.	Justice	500	498	0.52	**
6.	Total Moral Judgement	500	498	0.67	**

* Significant at 0.05 level

** Significant at 0.01 level

From the above table it can be seen that the obtained 'r' values 0.46, 0.57, 0.63, 0.71, 0.52 and 0.67 are higher than the table value 0.088 at 0.05 level and 0.115 at 0.01 level of significance. Therefore the null hypothesis was rejected at both levels of significance. The alternate hypothesis that there is significant and positive relationship between all dimensions of moral judgement of students and their Personality Traits (Ambiversion) is accepted.

<u>t-test Analysis</u>

Major Hypothesis

8. There is no significant difference in the different dimensions of moral judgement of students as per differences in their Parental Behaviour.

Minor Hypotheses

8.1. There is no significant difference in the honesty dimension of moral judgement of students as per differences in their Parental Behaviour.

8.2. There is no significant difference in the truthfulness dimension of moral judgement of students as per differences in their Parental Behaviour.

8.3. There is no significant difference in the non-violence dimension of moral judgement of students as per differences in their Parental Behaviour.

8.4. There is no significant difference in the obedience dimension of moral judgement of students as per differences in their Parental Behaviour.

8.5. There is no significant difference in the justice dimension of moral judgement of students as per differences in their Parental Behaviour.

8.6. There is no significant difference in the total moral judgement of students as per differences in their Parental Behaviour.

Table 4.8

Table showing the N, Mean, SD, 't' values of the different dimensions of Moral Judgement scores of students as per differences in their parental behaviour.

Sl. No.	Variables	N	Mean	S.D.	't' value	Level of Significance at 0.05 and 0.01
I.	Dimensions of Moral Judgement					
1.	Honesty					
	a) Low PB	247	15.17	5.03	14.54	**
	b) High PB	253	20.96	3.80		
2.	Truthfulness					
	a) Low PB	247	13.64	4.66	15.48	**
	b) High PB	253	19.08	3.03		
3.	Non-Violence					
	a) Low PB	247	14.85	4.85	14.70	**
	b) High PB	253	20.71	4.05		
4.	Obedience					
	a) Low PB	247	15.75	5.74	14.69	**
	b) High PB	253	22.91	5.14		
5.	Justice					
	a) Low PB	247	14.88	5.23	12.94	**
	b) High PB	253	20.48	4.41		
II.	Total Moral Judgement					
	a) Low PB	247	74.31	22.67	16.26	**
	b) High PB	253	104.17	18.20		

Note: PB = Parental Behaviour

** Significant at 0.01 level

Table 4.8 reveals that the obtained t-values for all the dimensions of Moral Judgement of students – honesty t = 14.54, truthfulness t = 15.48, non-violence t = 14.70, obedience t = 14.69, justice t = 12.94 and total Moral Judgement t = 16.26 are far above the table value which is 1.96 at 0.05 and 2.59 and 0.01 level and therefore are found significant at both 0.05 and 0.01 levels of significance. So the null hypothesis in this regard was rejected. The alternative hypothesis is formulated, that is, there is significant difference in all the dimensions of Moral Judgement of students as per their difference in their parental behaviour. Students with high parental behaviour M = 20.96, 19.08, 20.71, 22.91, 20.48 and 104.71 have higher levels of moral judgement on the total and all the dimensions of moral judgement than student with low parental behaviour.

Major Hypothesis

9. There is no significant difference in the different dimensions of Moral Judgement of students as per differences in their Father oriented Child Rearing Practices.

Minor Hypotheses

9.1. There is no significant difference in the honesty dimension of moral judgement of students as per differences in their Father oriented Child Rearing Practices.

9.2. There is no significant difference in the truthfulness dimension of moral judgement of students as per differences in their Father oriented Child Rearing Practices.

9.3. There is no significant difference in the non-violence dimension of moral judgement of students as per differences in their Father oriented Child Rearing Practices.

9.4. There is no significant difference in the obedience dimension of moral judgement of students as per differences in their Father oriented Child Rearing Practices.

9.5. There is no significant difference in the justice dimension of moral judgement of students as per differences in their Father oriented Child Rearing Practices.

9.6. There is no significant difference in the total moral judgement of students as per differences in their Father oriented Child Rearing Practices.

Table 4.9

Table showing the N, Mean, SD, 't' values of the different dimensions of Moral Judgement scores of students as per differences in their Father oriented Child Rearing Practices.

Sl. No.	Variables	N	Mean	S.D.	't' value	Level of Significance at 0.05 and 0.01
I.	Dimensions of Moral Judgement					
1.	Honesty					
	a) Low FCRP	216	15.37	5.21	11.23	**
	b) High FCRP	284	20.18	4.36		
2.	Truthfulness					
	a) Low FCRP	216	13.81	4.73	12.00	**
	b) High FCRP	284	18.36	3.76		
3.	Non-Violence					
	a) Low FCRP	216	14.88	4.98	12.18	**
	b) High FCRP	284	20.04	4.45		
4.	Obedience					
	a) Low FCRP	216	15.99	6.09	11.37	**
	b) High FCRP	284	21.95	5.59		

5.	Justice a) Low FCRP b) High FCRP	216 284	14.88 19.87	5.31 4.77	11.01	**
II.	Total Moral Judgement a) Low FCRP b) High FCRP	216 284	74.94 100.43	23.83 20.55	12.81	**

Note: FCRP = Father-oriented Child Rearing Practices

** Significant at 0.01 level

It is observed from the table 4.9 that the obtained t-values for all the dimensions of Moral Judgement of students, i.e., honesty t = 11.23, truthfulness t = 12.00, non-violence t = 12.18, obedience t = 11.37, justice t = 11.01 and total Moral Judgement t = 12.81 are far above the table value which is 1.96 and 2.59 at 0.05 and 0.01 levels respectively. So the null hypothesis in this regard was rejected. The alternative hypothesis was formulated, namely, there is significant difference in all the dimensions of Moral Judgement of students with regard to their high and low levels of father oriented child rearing practices. Students brought up with high level of father oriented child rearing practices, M = 100.73, 20.18, 18.36, 20.04, 21.95 and 19.87 had higher levels of moral judgement than students brought up with low levels of father oriented child rearing practices.

Major Hypothesis

10. There is no significant difference in the different dimensions of moral judgement of students as per differences in their Mother oriented Child Rearing Practices.

Minor Hypotheses

10.1. There is no significant difference in the honesty dimension of moral judgement of students as per differences in their Mother oriented Child Rearing Practices.

10.2. There is no significant difference in the truthfulness dimension of moral judgement of students as per differences in their Mother oriented Child Rearing Practices.

10.3. There is no significant difference in the non-violence dimension of moral judgement of students as per differences in their Mother oriented Child Rearing Practices.

10.4. There is no significant difference in the obedience dimension of moral judgement of students as per differences in their Mother oriented Child Rearing Practices.

10.5. There is no significant difference in the justice dimension of moral judgement of students as per differences in their Mother oriented Child Rearing Practices.

10.6. There is no significant difference in the total moral judgement of students as per differences in their Mother oriented Child Rearing Practices.

Table 4.10

Table showing the N, Mean, SD, 't' values of the different dimensions of Moral Judgement scores of students as per differences in their Mother oriented Child Rearing Practices.

Sl. No.	Variables	N	Mean	S.D.	't' value	Level of Significance at 0.05 and 0.01
I.	Dimensions of Moral Judgement					
1.	Honesty					
	a) Low MCRP	221	15.62	5.29	10.19	**
	b) High MCRP	279	20.06	4.43		
2.	Truthfulness					
	a) Low MCRP	221	13.94	4.77	11.52	**
	b) High MCRP	279	18.34	3.78		
3.	Non-Violence					
	a) Low MCRP	221	15.19	5.11	10.90	**
	b) High MCRP	279	19.90	4.54		
4.	Obedience					
	a) Low MCRP	221	16.30	6.20	10.33	**
	b) High MCRP	279	21.81	5.68		
5.	Justice					
	a) Low MCRP	221	15.19	5.48	9.82	**
	b) High MCRP	279	19.72	4.81		
II.	Total Moral Judgement					
	a) Low MCRP	221	76.26	24.42	11.63	**
	b) High MCRP	279	99.84	20.91		

Note: MCRP = Mother-oriented Child Rearing Practices

** Significant at 0.01 level

The obtained results observed from table 4.10 reveals that all the t-values for the dimensions of Moral Judgement, i.e., honesty t = 10.19, truthfulness t = 11.52, non-violence t = 10.90, obedience t = 10.33, justice t = 9.82 and total Moral Judgement t = 11.63 are far above the table value which is 1.96 and 2.59 at 0.05 and 0.01 levels of probability respectively. So the null hypothesis in this regard was rejected. The alternative hypotheses was formulated that is, there is significant difference in all the dimensions of Moral Judgement of students as per differences in their levels of mother oriented child rearing practices. Students brought up with high level mother oriented behaviour had higher levels of moral judgement than students brought up with low levels of mother oriented child rearing practices. This conclusion was reached after observing the means of high mother oriented child rearing practices which was higher in all dimensions of Moral Judgement than low mother oriented child rearing practices.

Major Hypothesis

11. There is no significant difference in the different dimensions of moral judgement of students as per differences in their Self knowledge component of Emotional Maturity.

Minor Hypotheses

11.1. There is no significant difference in the honesty dimension of moral judgement of students as per differences in their Self knowledge component of Emotional Maturity.

11.2. There is no significant difference in the truthfulness dimension of moral judgement of students as per differences in their Self knowledge component of Emotional Maturity.

11.3. There is no significant difference in the non-violence dimension of moral judgement of students as per differences in their Self knowledge component of Emotional Maturity.

11.4. There is no significant difference in the obedience dimension of moral judgement of students as per differences in their Self knowledge component of Emotional Maturity.

11.5. There is no significant difference in the justice dimension of moral judgement of students as per differences in their Self knowledge component of Emotional Maturity.

11.6. There is no significant difference in the total moral judgement of students as per differences in their Self knowledge component of Emotional Maturity.

Table 4.11

Table showing the N, Mean, SD, 't' values of the different dimensions of Moral Judgement scores of students as per differences in their Self knowledge component of Emotional Maturity.

Sl. No.	Variables	N	Mean	S.D.	't' value	Level of Significance at 0.05 and 0.01
I.	Dimensions of Moral Judgement					
1.	Honesty					
	a) Low SK	315	15.18	4.93	16.56	**
	b) High SK	185	22.22	2.76		
2.	Truthfulness					
	a) Low SK	315	13.94	4.77	14.85	**
	b) High SK	185	19.84	2.48		
3.	Non-Violence					
	a) Low SK	315	15.30	4.78	17.45	**
	b) High SK	185	22.10	2.97		
4.	Obedience					
	a) Low SK	315	16.20	5.76	18.36	**
	b) High SK	185	24.77	3.47		
5.	Justice					
	a) Low SK	315	15.15	5.06	16.76	**
	b) High SK	185	22.09	3.22		
II.	Total Moral Judgement					
	a) Low SK	315	76.72	22.07	19.28	**
	b) High SK	185	111.05	12.97		

SK = Self-knowledge

** Significant at 0.01 level

Table 4.11 reveals that the obtained t-values (16.56, 14.85, 17.45, 18.36, 16.76 and 19.28) for all the dimensions of Moral Judgement and total Moral Judgement are far above the table value which is 1.96 and 2.59 at 0.05 and 0.01 levels of significance respectively. So the null hypothesis was rejected. This means that there is significant difference in the Moral Judgement of students as per differences in their levels of self knowledge. Students possessing high level of self knowledge had higher level of Moral Judgement than students possessing low self knowledge. An observation of the means of high and low levels of self knowledge of students confirmed the above interpretation.

Major Hypothesis

12. There is no significant difference in the different dimensions of moral judgement of students as per differences in their Self Confidence component of Emotional Maturity.

Minor Hypotheses

12.1. There is no significant difference in the honesty dimension of moral judgement of students as per differences in their Self Confidence component of Emotional Maturity.

12.2. There is no significant difference in the truthfulness dimension of moral judgement of students as per differences in their Self Confidence component of Emotional Maturity.

12.3. There is no significant difference in the non-violence dimension of moral judgement of students as per differences in their Self Confidence component of Emotional Maturity.

12.4. There is no significant difference in the obedience dimension of moral judgement of students as per differences in their Self Confidence component of Emotional Maturity.

12.5. There is no significant difference in the justice dimension of moral judgement of students as per differences in their Self Confidence component of Emotional Maturity.

12.6. There is no significant difference in the total moral judgement of students as per differences in their Self Confidence component of Emotional Maturity.

Table 4.12

Table showing the N, Mean, SD, 't' values of the different dimensions of Moral Judgement scores of students as per differences in their Self Confidence component of Emotional Maturity.

Sl. No.	Variables	N	Mean	S.D.	't' value	Level of Significance at 0.05 and 0.01
I.	Dimensions of Moral Judgement					
1.	Honesty					
	a) Low SCF	282	14.93	4.58	20.71	**
	b) High SCF	218	22.20	2.76		
2.	Truthfulness					
	a) Low SCF	282	13.65	4.36	19.26	**
	b) High SCF	218	19.94	2.31		
3.	Non-Violence					
	a) Low SCF	282	14.54	4.42	21.75	**
	b) High SCF	218	22.05	2.86		
4.	Obedience					
	a) Low SCF	282	15.13	4.96	24.66	**
	b) High SCF	218	24.87	3.46		
5.	Justice					
	a) Low SCF	282	14.33	4.59	21.29	**
	b) High SCF	218	22.10	3.19		
II.	Total Moral Judgement					
	a) Low SCF	282	72.60	19.27	25.65	**
	b) High SCF	218	111.17	12.52		

SCF = Self-Confidence

** Significant at 0.01 level

Table 4.12 depicts that the obtained t-values for all the dimensions of Moral Judgement, i.e., honesty t = 20.71, truthfulness t = 19.26, non-violence t = 21.75, obedience t = 24.66, justice t = 21.29 and total Moral Judgement t = 25.65 are far above the table value which is 1.96 and 2.59 at 0.05 and 0.10 levels of significance respectively. So the null hypothesis was rejected. The alternative hypothesis was formulated that is there is significant difference in the Moral Judgement of students as per differences in their levels of self-confidence component of Emotional Maturity. Students having a higher level of self confidence had higher levels of Moral Judgement than students having low levels of self confidence. Observation of the means of high and low self confidence groups of students enabled the investigator to arrive at this interpretation since the means of high self confidence groups was higher than the means of low self confidence groups on all the dimensions of Moral Judgement.

Major Hypothesis

13. There is no significant difference in the different dimensions of moral judgement of students as per differences in their Acceptance of Reality Component of Emotional Maturity.

Minor Hypotheses

13.1. There is no significant difference in the honesty dimension of moral judgement of students as per differences in their Acceptance of Reality Component of Emotional Maturity.

13.2. There is no significant difference in the truthfulness dimension of moral judgement of students as per differences in their Acceptance of Reality Component of Emotional Maturity.

13.3. There is no significant difference in the non-violence dimension of moral judgement of students as per differences in their Acceptance of Reality Component of Emotional Maturity.

13.4. There is no significant difference in the obedience dimension of moral judgement of students as per differences in their Acceptance of Reality Component of Emotional Maturity.

13.5. There is no significant difference in the justice dimension of moral judgement of students as per differences in their Acceptance of Reality Component of Emotional Maturity.

13.6. There is no significant difference in the total moral judgement of students as per differences in their Acceptance of Reality Component of Emotional Maturity.

Table 4.13

Table showing the N, Mean, SD, 't' values of the different dimensions of Moral Judgement scores of students as per differences in their Acceptance of Reality Component of Emotional Maturity.

Sl. No.	Variables	N	Mean	S.D.	't' value	Level of Significance at 0.05 and 0.01
I.	Dimensions of Moral Judgement					
1.	Honesty					
	a) Low AR	224	14.58	4.98	16.61	**
	b) High AR	276	20.95	3.57		
2.	Truthfulness					
	a) Low AR	224	13.01	4.58	18.52	**
	b) High AR	276	19.14	2.73		
3.	Non-Violence					
	a) Low AR	224	13.95	4.59	19.18	**
	b) High AR	276	20.95	3.55		
4.	Obedience					
	a) Low AR	224	15.10	5.77	16.36	**
	b) High AR	276	22.8	4.81		
5.	Justice					
	a) Low AR	224	14.04	5.01	16.42	**
	b) High AR	276	20.69	4.04		
II.	Total Moral Judgement					
	a) Low AR	224	70.72	22.40	19.84	**
	b) High AR	276	104.60	15.66		

AR = Acceptance of Reality ** Significant at 0.01 level

Table 4.13 indicates that the obtained t-values (t = 16.61, 18.52, 19.18, 16.36, 16.42 and 19.84) for all the dimensions of Moral Judgement and total Moral Judgement are far above the table value which is 1.96 and 2.59 at 0.05 and 0.01 levels of significance respectively. So the null hypothesis was rejected and the alternative hypothesis was formulated that there is significant difference in the Moral Judgement of students as per differences in the levels of Acceptance of Reality. Students having high level of Acceptance of Reality had better Moral Judgement than students having low level of Acceptance of Reality. Since the means of the former was higher than the means of the latter this interpretation was stated thus.

Major Hypothesis

14. There is no significant difference in the different dimensions of moral judgement of students as per differences in their Self Control Component of Emotional Maturity.

Minor Hypotheses

14.1. There is no significant difference in the honesty dimension of moral judgement of students as per differences in their Self Control component of Emotional Maturity.

14.2. There is no significant difference in the truthfulness dimension of moral judgement of students as per differences in their Self Control component of Emotional Maturity.

14.3. There is no significant difference in the non-violence dimension of moral judgement of students as per differences in their Self Control component of Emotional Maturity.

14.4. There is no significant difference in the obedience dimension of moral judgement of students as per differences in their Self Control component of Emotional Maturity.

14.5. There is no significant difference in the justice dimension of moral judgement of students as per differences in their Self Control component of Emotional Maturity.

14.6. There is no significant difference in the total moral judgement of students as per differences in their Self Control component of Emotional Maturity.

Table 4.14

Table showing the N, Mean, SD, 't' values of the different dimensions of Moral Judgement scores of students as per differences in their Self Control component of Emotional Maturity.

Sl. No.	Variables	N	Mean	S.D.	't' value	Level of Significance at 0.05 and 0.01
I.	Dimensions of Moral Judgement					
1.	Honesty					
	a) Low SCT	282	14.69	4.45	23.92	**
	b) High SCT	218	22.51	2.10		
2.	Truthfulness					
	a) Low SCT	282	13.45	4.30	22.02	**
	b) High SCT	218	20.21	2.48		
3.	Non-Violence					
	a) Low SCT	282	14.40	4.41	23.77	**
	b) High SCT	218	22.24	2.35		
4.	Obedience					
	a) Low SCT	282	15.10	4.99	24.99	**
	b) High SCT	218	24.90	3.33		
5.	Justice					
	a) Low SCT	282	14.03	4.37	25.44	**
	b) High SCT	218	22.49	2.53		
II.	Total Moral Judgement					
	a) Low SCT	282	71.69	18.87	29.30	**
	b) High SCT	218	112.36	9.09		

SCT = Self Control Component

** Significant at 0.01 level

From table 4.14 it is observed that the t-values for all the dimensions of Moral Judgement, i.e., honesty t = 23.92, truthfulness t = 22.02, non-violence t = 23.77, obedience t = 24.99, justice t = 25.44 and total Moral Judgement are far above the table value which is 1.96 and 2.59 at 0.05 and 0.01 levels of significance respectively. Therefore the null hypothesis was rejected. This means that there is significant difference in the Moral Judgement of students as per differences in the levels of self control. Students with high level of self control had better Moral Judgement than students with low self control.

Major Hypothesis

15. There is no significant difference in the different dimensions of moral judgement of students as per differences in their Social Adjustment Component of Emotional Maturity.

Minor Hypotheses

15.1. There is no significant difference in the honesty dimension of moral judgement of students as per differences in their Social Adjustment component of Emotional Maturity.

15.2. There is no significant difference in the truthfulness dimension of moral judgement of students as per differences in their Social Adjustment component of Emotional Maturity.

15.3. There is no significant difference in the non-violence dimension of moral judgement of students as per differences in their Social Adjustment component of Emotional Maturity.

15.4. There is no significant difference in the obedience dimension of moral judgement of students as per differences in their Social Adjustment component of Emotional Maturity.

15.5. There is no significant difference in the justice dimension of moral judgement of students as per differences in their Social Adjustment component of Emotional Maturity.

15.6. There is no significant difference in the total moral judgement of students as per differences in their Social Adjustment component of Emotional Maturity.

Table 4.15

Table showing the N, Mean, SD, 't' values of the different dimensions of Moral Judgement scores of students as per differences in their Social Adjustment component of Emotional Maturity.

Sl. No.	Variables	N	Mean	S.D.	't' value	Level of Significance at 0.05 and 0.01
I.	Dimensions of Moral Judgement					
1.	Honesty					
	a) Low SA	318	15.54	4.79	18.46	**
	b) High SA	182	22.57	2.43		
2.	Truthfulness					
	a) Low SA	318	14.20	4.58	17.15	**
	b) High SA	182	20.24	1.65		
3.	Non-Violence					
	a) Low SA	318	15.10	4.64	20.13	**
	b) High SA	182	22.56	2.28		
4.	Obedience					
	a) Low SA	318	15.97	5.47	21.38	**
	b) High SA	182	25.33	2.92		
5.	Justice					
	a) Low SA	318	14.97	4.89	19.10	**
	b) High SA	182	22.51	2.76		
II.	Total Moral Judgement					
	a) Low SA	318	75.79	21.07	22.52	**
	b) High SA	182	113.23	10.09		

SA: Social Adjustment

** Significant at 0.01 level

Table 4.15 indicates that the obtained t-values (18.46, 17.15, 20.13, 21.38, 19.10 and 22.32) for all the dimensions of Moral Judgement and total Moral Judgement are far above the table value which is 1.96 and 2.59 at 0.05 and 0.01 levels of significance respectively. Therefore, the null hypothesis is rejected in this regard and the alternative hypothesis is accepted namely that there is a significance difference in the different dimensions of Moral Judgement of students as per differences in their social adjustment. The table further reveals that students having high levels of social adjustment have better Moral Judgement than students have low social adjustment. This interpretation was arrived at after examining the means of high social adjustment groups which was higher than the low social adjustment group.

Major Hypothesis

16. There is no significant difference in the different dimensions of moral judgement of students as per differences in their Consistency Component of Emotional Maturity.

Minor Hypotheses

16.1. There is no significant difference in the honesty dimension of moral judgement of students as per differences in their Consistency component of Emotional Maturity.

16.2. There is no significant difference in the truthfulness dimension of moral judgement of students as per differences in their Consistency component of Emotional Maturity.

16.3. There is no significant difference in the non-violence dimension of moral judgement of students as per differences in their Consistency component of Emotional Maturity.

16.4. There is no significant difference in the obedience dimension of moral judgement of students as per differences in their Consistency component of Emotional Maturity.

16.5. There is no significant difference in the justice dimension of moral judgement of students as per differences in their Consistency component of Emotional Maturity.

16.6. There is no significant difference in the total moral judgement of students as per differences in their Consistency component of Emotional Maturity.

Table 4.16

Table showing the N, Mean, SD, 't' values of the different dimensions of Moral Judgement scores of students as per differences in their Consistency Component of Emotional Maturity.

Sl. No.	Variables	N	Mean	S.D.	't' value	Level of Significance at 0.05 and 0.01
I.	Dimensions of Moral Judgement					
1.	Honesty					
	a) Low Consistency	221	13.80	4.18	23.30	**
	b) High Consistency	279	21.51	3.21		
2.	Truthfulness					
	a) Low Consistency	221	12.41	4.08	24.86	**
	b) High Consistency	279	19.55	2.25		
3.	Non-Violence					
	a) Low Consistency	221	13.38	4.18	24.60	**
	b) High Consistency	279	21.33	3.04		
4.	Obedience					
	a) Low Consistency	221	13.95	4.71	24.71	**
	b) High Consistency	279	23.68	4.07		
5.	Justice					
	a) Low Consistency	221	13.14	4.02	23.87	**
	b) High Consistency	279	21.34	3.64		
II.	Total Moral Judgement					
	a) Low Consistency	221	66.68	17.57	29.58	**
	b) High Consistency	279	107.43	13.22		

** Significant at 0.01 level

Table 4.16 indicates that the obtained t-values for all the dimensions of Moral Judgement, i.e., honesty t = 23.30, truthfulness t = 24.86, non-violence t = 24.60, obedience t = 24.71, justice t = 23.87 and total Moral Judgement t = 29.58 are far above the table value which is 1.96 and 2.59 at 0.05 and 0.01 levels of significance respectively. Therefore, the null hypothesis in this regard is rejected. The alternative hypothesis that there is significant difference in the Moral Judgement of students as per differences in their Consistency is formulated. The table further reveals that students with high consistency have better Moral Judgement than students with low consistency. The means of the high consistency group of students is higher than the means of low consistency group of students thereby helping the investigator at arriving at this interpretation.

Major Hypothesis

17. There is no significant difference in the different dimensions of Moral Judgement of students as per differences in their total Emotional Maturity.

Minor Hypotheses

17.1. There is no significant difference in the honesty dimension of moral judgement of students as per differences in their Total Emotional Maturity.

17.2. There is no significant difference in the truthfulness dimension of moral judgement of students as per differences in their Total Emotional Maturity.

17.3. There is no significant difference in the non-violence dimension of moral judgement of students as per differences in their Total Emotional Maturity.

17.4. There is no significant difference in the obedience dimension of moral judgement of students as per differences in their Total Emotional Maturity.

17.5. There is no significant difference in the justice dimension of moral judgement of students as per differences in their Total Emotional Maturity.

17.6. There is no significant difference in the total moral judgement of students as per differences in their Total Emotional Maturity.

Table 4.17

Table showing the N, Mean, SD, 't' values of the different dimensions of Moral Judgement scores of students as per differences in their total Emotional Maturity.

Sl. No.	Variables	N	Mean	S.D.	't' value	Level of Significance at 0.05 and 0.01
I.	Dimensions of Moral Judgement					
1.	Honesty					
	a) Low EMT	271	14.33	4.17	27.26	**
	b) High EMT	229	22.56	2.02		
2.	Truthfulness					
	a) Low EMT	271	13.23	4.22	23.31	**
	b) High EMT	229	20.14	1.65		
3.	Non-Violence					
	a) Low EMT	271	14.10	4.21	25.86	**
	b) High EMT	229	22.21	2.37		
4.	Obedience					
	a) Low EMT	271	14.70	4.21	27.97	**
	b) High EMT	229	22.21	2.37		
5.	Justice					
	a) Low EMT	271	13.76	4.20	27.10	**
	b) High EMT	229	22.40	2.57		
II.	Total Moral Judgement					
	a) Low EMT	271	10.13	17.53	32.92	**
	b) High EMT	229	112.25	8.93		

EMT = Total Emotional Maturity

** Significant at 0.01 level

Table 4.17 indicates that the obtained t-value for all the dimensions of Moral Judgement, i.e., honesty t = 27.26, truthfulness t = 23.31, non-violence t = 25.86, obedience t = 27.97, justice t = 27.10 and total Moral Judgement t = 32.92 are far above the table value which is 1.96 and 2.59 at 0.05 and 0.01 levels of significance. Therefore, the null hypothesis in this regard is rejected and the alternative hypothesis is formulated that there is a significant difference in the Moral Judgement of students as per differences in their Emotional Maturity. The table further reveals that students with high level of emotional maturity have better Moral Judgement on all the dimensions than students with low emotional maturity.

Major Hypothesis

18. There is no significant difference in the different dimensions of moral judgement of students as per differences in their personality traits (Extroverts, Introverts and Ambiverts).

Minor Hypotheses

18.1. There is no significant difference in the honesty dimension of moral judgement of Extroverted and Introverted students.

18.2. There is no significant difference in the truthfulness dimension of moral judgement of Extroverted and Introverted students.

18.3. There is no significant difference in the non-violence dimension of moral judgement of Extroverted and Introverted students.

18.4. There is no significant difference in the obedience dimension of moral judgement of Extroverted and Introverted students.

18.5. There is no significant difference in the justice dimension of moral judgement of Extroverted and Introverted students.

18.6. There is no significant difference in the total moral judgement of Extroverted and Introverted students.

Table 4.18

Table showing the N, Mean, SD, 't' values of the different dimensions of Moral Judgement scores of students as per differences in their personality traits (Extrovert-Introvert).

Sl. No.	Variables	N	Mean	S.D.	't' value	Level of Significance at 0.05 and 0.01
I.	Dimensions of Moral Judgement					
1.	Honesty					
	a) Extrovert	212	17.45	5.29	1.44	NS
	b) Introvert	209	18.20	5.34		
2.	Truthfulness					
	a) Extrovert	212	15.99	4.81	1.11	NS
	b) Introvert	209	16.51	4.75		
3.	Non-Violence					
	a) Extrovert	212	17.65	5.39	0.05	NS
	b) Introvert	209	17.67	5.28		
4.	Obedience					
	a) Extrovert	212	18.89	6.46	0.73	NS
	b) Introvert	209	19.35	6.53		
5.	Justice					
	a) Extrovert	212	17.10	5.77	1.37	NS
	b) Introvert	209	17.85	5.30		
II.	Total Moral Judgement					
	a) Extrovert	212	87.10	25.26	1.01	NS
	b) Introvert	209	89.60	25.30		

** Significant at 0.01 level NS = Not Significant
* Significant at 0.05 level

Table 4.18 reveals that the obtained t-values 1.44, 1.11, 0.05, 0.73, 1.37 and 1.01 for all the dimensions of total Moral Judgement were far below the table value of 1.96 at 0.05 level of significance. Therefore the null hypothesis is accepted that there is no significant difference in the Moral Judgement of extroverted and introverted students.

Minor Hypotheses

18.7. There is no significant difference in the honesty dimension of moral judgement of Extroverted and Ambiverted students.

18.8. There is no significant difference in the truthfulness dimension of moral judgement of Extroverted and Ambiverted students.

18.9. There is no significant difference in the non-violence dimension of moral judgement of Extroverted and Ambiverted students.

18.10. There is no significant difference in the obedience dimension of moral judgement of Extroverted and Ambiverted students.

18.11. There is no significant difference in the justice dimension of moral judgement of Extroverted and Ambiverted students.

18.12. There is no significant difference in the total moral judgement of Extroverted and Ambiverted students.

Table 4.19

Table showing the N, Mean, SD, 't' values of the different dimensions of Moral Judgement scores of students as per differences in their personality traits (Extrovert-Ambivert).

Sl. No.	Variable	N	Mean	S.D.	't' value	Level of Significance at 0.05 and 0.01
I.	Dimensions of Moral Judgement					
1.	Honesty					
	a) Extrovert	212	17.45	5.29	3.07	*
	b) Ambivert	79	19.56	5.00		
2.	Truthfulness					
	a) Extrovert	212	15.99	4.81	1.90	NS
	b) Ambivert	79	17.18	4.66		
3.	Non-Violence					
	a) Extrovert	212	17.65	5.39	1.40	NS
	b) Ambivert	79	18.64	5.33		
4.	Obedience					
	a) Extrovert	212	18.89	6.46	2.19	*
	b) Ambivert	79	20.75	6.50		
5.	Justice					
	a) Extrovert	212	17.10	5.77	2.52	*
	b) Ambivert	79	19.01	5.60		
II.	Total Moral Judgement					
	a) Extrovert	212	87.10	25.26	2.42	*
	b) Ambivert	79	95.17	25.25		

** Significant at 0.01 level

* Significant at 0.05 level

NS = Not Significant

Table 4.19 reveals that the obtained t-values 3.07, 2.19, 2.52 and 2.42 were above the table value of 1.96 at 0.05 level of significance. Therefore the null hypothesis was rejected and the alternate hypothesis that there is significant difference in the honesty, obedience, justice dimensions of Moral Judgement and total Moral Judgement of extroverted and ambiverted students. Students with ambivert type of personality (M = 19.56, 20.75, 19.01 and 95.17) had higher levels of Moral Judgement than students belonging to extrovert type of personality. However the t-values for the remaining 2 dimensions of Moral Judgement, namely, truthfulness and non violence was found to be far below the table value 1.96 at 0.05 level of significance and hence not significant. The null hypothesis in this regard has been accepted.

Minor Hypotheses

18.13. There is no significant difference in the honesty dimension of moral judgement of Introverted and Ambiverted students.

18.14. There is no significant difference in the truthfulness dimension of moral judgement of Introverted and Ambiverted students.

18.15. There is no significant difference in the non-violence dimension of moral judgement of Introverted and Ambiverted students.

18.16. There is no significant difference in the obedience dimension of moral judgement of Introverted and Ambiverted students.

18.17. There is no significant difference in the justice dimension of moral judgement of Introverted and Ambiverted students.

18.18. There is no significant difference in the total moral judgement of Introverted and Ambiverted students.

Table 4.20

Table showing the N, Mean, SD, 't' values of the different dimensions of Moral Judgement scores of students as per differences in their personality traits (Ambivert-Introvert).

Sl. No.	Variable	N	Mean	S.D.	't' value	Level of Significance at 0.05 and 0.01
I.	Dimensions of Moral Judgement					
1.	Honesty					
	a) Ambivert	79	19.56	5.00	1.97	NS
	b) Introvert	209	18.20	5.34		
2.	Truthfulness					
	a) Ambivert	79	17.18	4.66	1.08	NS
	b) Introvert	209	16.51	4.75		
3.	Non-Violence					
	a) Ambivert	79	18.64	5.33	1.38	NS
	b) Introvert	209	17.67	5.28		
4.	Obedience					
	a) Ambivert	79	20.75	6.50	1.63	NS
	b) Introvert	209	19.35	6.53		
5.	Justice					
	a) Ambivert	79	19.01	5.60	1.63	NS
	b) Introvert	209	17.85	5.30		
II.	Total Moral Judgement					
	a) Ambivert	79	95.17	25.25	1.67	NS
	b) Introvert	209	89.60	25.30		

** Significant at 0.01 level

* Significant at 0.05 level

NS = Not Significant

Table 4.20 reveals that the obtained t-values 1.97, 1.08, 1.38, 1.63, 1.63 and 1.67 for all the dimensions and total Moral Judgement were far below the table value of 1.96 at 0.05 level of significance. Therefore the null hypothesis was accepted that there is no significant difference in the Moral Judgement of ambiverted and introverted students.

Major Hypothesis

19. There is no significant difference in the different dimensions of moral judgement of students as per differences in their parents' socio-economic status.

Minor Hypotheses

19.1. There is no significant difference in the honesty dimension of moral judgement of students as per differences in their Parents' socio-economic status.

19.2. There is no significant difference in the truthfulness dimension of moral judgement of students as per differences in their Parents' socio-economic status.

19.3. There is no significant difference in the non-violence dimension of moral judgement of students as per differences in their Parents' socio-economic status.

19.4. There is no significant difference in the obedience dimension of moral judgement of students as per differences in their Parents' socio-economic status.

19.5. There is no significant difference in the justice dimension of moral judgement of students as per differences in their Parents' socio-economic status.

19.6. There is no significant difference in the total moral judgement of students as per differences in their Parents' socio-economic status.

Table 4.21

Table showing the N, Mean, SD, 't' values of the different dimensions of Moral Judgement scores of students as per differences in their parents socio-economic status.

Sl. No.	Variables	N	Mean	S.D.	't' value	Level of Significance at 0.05 and 0.01
I.	Dimensions of Moral Judgement					
1.	Honesty					
	a) Low SES	244	18.20	5.27	0.40	NS
	b) High SES	256	22.56	2.02		
2.	Truthfulness					
	a) Low SES	244	16.59	4.68	0.91	NS
	b) High SES	256	16.21	4.85		
3.	Non-Violence					
	a) Low SES	244	17.90	5.34	0.35	NS
	b) High SES	256	17.73	5.35		
4.	Obedience					
	a) Low SES	244	19.46	6.60	0.29	NS
	b) High SES	256	19.29	6.44		
5.	Justice					
	a) Low SES	244	17.65	5.68	0.25	NS
	b) High SES	256	17.78	5.49		
II.	Total Moral Judgement					
	a) Low SES	244	89.82	25.46	0.35	NS
	b) High SES	256	89.03	25.34		

SES = Socio Economic Status

NS = Not Significant

Table 4.21 shows that the obtained t-value for all the dimensions of Moral Judgement and total are far below the table value which is 1.96 significant at 0.05 level of significance. So the null hypothesis was accepted. This clearly shows that there is no significant difference in the Moral Judgement of students belonging to high and low socio economic status groups.

Johnston (1981), Kalra (1978), Lewis (1982) and Mohundro (1976) are all of the opinion that socio-economic status was positively related with the level of moral judgement. But Evans (1980) came to

the conclusion that socio economic status has no relationship with moral judgement which is in line with the findings of the present study.

Major Hypothesis

20. There is no significant difference in the different dimensions of moral judgement of students as per differences in their sex.

Minor Hypotheses

20.1. There is no significant difference in the honesty dimension of moral judgement of students as per differences in their sex.

20.2. There is no significant difference in the truthfulness dimension of moral judgement of students as per differences in their sex.

20.3. There is no significant difference in the non-violence dimension of moral judgement of students as per differences in their sex.

20.4. There is no significant difference in the obedience dimension of moral judgement of students as per differences in their sex.

20.5. There is no significant difference in the justice dimension of moral judgement of students as per differences in their sex.

20.6. There is no significant difference in the total moral judgement of students as per differences in their sex.

Table 4.22

Table showing the N, Mean, SD, 't' values of the different dimensions of Moral Judgement of students as per differences in their sex.

Sl. No.	Variables	N	Mean	SD	't' value	Level of Significance at 0.05 and 0.01
I	Dimensions of Moral Judgement					
1.	Honesty a) Female b) Male	 250 250	 18.91 17.29	 5.22 5.27	 3.44	 **
2.	Truthfullness a) Female b) Male	 250 250	 17.26 17.29	 5.53 5.27	 4.11	 **
3.	Non-Violence a) Female b) Male	 250 250	 18.00 17.29	 5.43 5.27	 0.77	 NS
4.	Obedience a) Female b) Male	 250 250	 19.94 18.81	 6.75 6.23	 1.94	 NS
5.	Justice a) Female b) Male	 250 250	 17.95 17.48	 5.38 5.78	 0.94	 NS
II	Total Moral Judgement a) Female b) Male	250 250	92.08 86.76	25.46 25.06	2.35	*

** Significant at 0.01 level   * Significant at 0.05 level
NS = Not Significant

Table 4.22 reveals that the obtained t-value for the honesty dimension (t = 3.44) and truthfulness dimensions (t = 4.11) are both far above the table value which is 1.96 and 2.59 at 0.05 and 0.01 levels of significance respectively. So the null hypothesis with regard to the above was rejected. The alternate hypothesis is accepted that there is significant difference in the honesty and truthfulness dimension of Moral Judgement of students as per differences in their sex. However the t-values for the remaining 3 dimensions of Moral Judgement, namely, non-violence, obedience, justice was found to be far below the table value 1.96 at 0.05 level of significance and hence not significant. The null hypothesis in this regard has been accepted.

The table also reveals that the obtained t-value 2.35 for the total Moral Judgement is far above the table value of 1.96 at 0.05 level of significance. Therefore it is significant and the null hypothesis is rejected. The alternative hypothesis is formulated namely that there is significant difference in the Moral Judgement of male and female students.

Gopalaiah (1981) concluded that moral judgement did not depend on sex which is not in line with the present study which says that girls have higher moral judgement scores than boys. But Sony (1984) conducted a study of moral judgement of school going children of rural areas belonging to different sexes. The major finding of the study was that girls were better than boys in moral judgement, which coincides with the present study. Bush (1981), Kipust (1983), Kenvin (1981), Toai Ton (1978) Seifung (1981) and Fefis (1978) also conclude that there is no such significant difference in sex which accounted for significant difference in moral judgement. But Schunrer (1976) concluded that males were better than females in moral judgement.

Major Hypothesis

21. There is no significant difference in the different dimensions of moral judgement of students as per differences in the type of management in which they are studying.

Minor Hypotheses

21.1. There is no significant difference in the honesty dimension of moral judgement of students studying in government and aided schools.

21.2. There is no significant difference in the truthfulness dimension of moral judgement of students studying in government and aided schools.

21.3. There is no significant difference in the non-violence dimension of moral judgement of students studying in government and aided schools.

21.4. There is no significant difference in the obedience dimension of moral judgement of students studying in government and aided schools.

21.5. There is no significant difference in the justice dimension of moral judgement of students studying in government and aided schools.

21.6. There is no significant difference in the total moral judgement of students studying in government and aided schools.

Table 4.23

Table showing the N, Mean, SD, 't' values of the different dimensions of Moral Judgement scores of students studying in government and private aided schools.

Sl. No.	Variables	N	Mean	S.D.	't' value	Level of Significance at 0.05 and 0.01
I.	Dimensions of Moral Judgement					
1.	Honesty					
	a) Government	169	17.76	5.20	0.31	NS
	b) Aided	161	17.59	5.32		
2.	Truthfulness					
	a) Government	169	16.17	4.61	0.47	NS
	b) Aided	161	15.92	4.94		
3.	Non-Violence					
	a) Government	169	17.60	5.11	0.11	NS
	b) Aided	161	17.54	5.24		

4.	Obedience a) Government b) Aided	169 161	19.05 18.94	6.50 6.21	0.16	NS
5.	Justice a) Government b) Aided	169 161	17.22 17.72	5.66 5.38	0.82	NS
II.	Total Moral Judgement a) Government b) Aided	169 161	87.83 87.73	24.45 25.18	0.04	NS

** Significant at 0.01 level

* Significant at 0.05 level

NS = Not Significant

Table 4.23 reveals that the obtained t-value for all the dimension of Moral Judgement 0.31, 0.47, 0.11, 0.16, 0.82 and 0.04 are less than the table value which is 1.97 and 2.59 at 0.05 and 0.01 levels of significance respectively. Therefore the null hypotheses in this regard was accepted that there is no significant difference in the Moral Judgement of students studying in government and private aided schools.

Minor Hypotheses

21.7. There is no significant difference in the honesty dimension of moral judgement of students studying in government and unaided schools.

21.8. There is no significant difference in the truthfulness dimension of moral judgement of students studying in government and unaided schools.

21.9. There is no significant difference in the non-violence dimension of moral judgement of students studying in government and unaided schools.

21.10. There is no significant difference in the obedience dimension of moral judgement of students studying in government and unaided schools.

21.11. There is no significant difference in the justice dimension of moral judgement of students studying in government and unaided schools.

21.12. There is no significant difference in the total moral judgement of students studying in government and unaided schools.

Table 4.24

Table showing the N, Mean, SD, 't' values of the different dimensions of Moral Judgement scores of students studying in government and unaided schools.

Sl. No.	Variables	N	Mean	S.D.	't' value	Level of Significance at 0.05 and 0.01
I.	Dimensions of Moral Judgement					
1.	Honesty a) Government b) Unaided	169 170	17.76 18.92	5.20 5.33	2.02	*
2.	Truthfulness a) Government b) Unaided	169 170	16.17 17.07	4.61 4.72	1.78	NS
3.	Non-Violence a) Government b) Unaided	169 170	17.60 18.28	5.11 5.63	1.16	NS
4.	Obedience a) Government b) Unaided	169 170	19.05 20.11	6.50 6.78	1.46	NS
5.	Justice a) Government b) Unaided	169 170	17.22 18.20	5.66 5.67	1.59	NS
II.	Total Moral Judgement a) Government b) Unaided	169 170	87.83 92.60	24.45 26.28	1.59	NS

* Significant at 0.05 level

NS = Not Significant

It is observed from the table 4.24 that the t-value for honesty dimension t = 2.02 was above the table value which is 1.97 at 0.05 level of significance, the rest of the t-values were not significant at both the levels. The null hypothesis in case of honesty dimension was rejected and the alternate hypothesis is formulated that is there is significant difference in the honesty component of Moral Judgement of students studying in government and unaided type of schools. In the case of the remaining dimensions of Moral Judgement the hypothesis was accepted.

Minor Hypotheses

21.13. There is no significant difference in the honesty dimension of moral judgement of students studying in private aided and private unaided schools.

21.14. There is no significant difference in the truthfulness dimension of moral judgement of students studying in private aided and private unaided schools.

21.15. There is no significant difference in the non-violence dimension of moral judgement of students studying in private aided and private unaided schools.

21.16. There is no significant difference in the obedience dimension of moral judgement of students studying in private aided and private unaided schools.

21.17. There is no significant difference in the justice dimension of moral judgement of students studying in private aided and private unaided schools.

21.18. There is no significant difference in the total moral judgement of students studying in private aided and private unaided schools.

Table 4.25

Table showing the N, Mean, SD, 't' values of the different dimensions of Moral Judgement scores of students studying in private aided and unaided schools.

Sl. No.	Variables	N	Mean	S.D.	't' value	Level of Significance at 0.05 and 0.01
I.	Dimensions of Moral Judgement					
1.	Honesty					
	a) Private Aided	161	17.59	5.32	2.28	*
	b) Private Unaided	170	18.92	5.33		
2.	Truthfulness					
	a) Private Aided	161	15.92	4.94	0.47	NS
	b) Private Unaided	170	17.07	4.72		
3.	Non-Violence					
	a) Private Aided	161	17.54	5.24	1.24	NS
	b) Private Unaided	170	18.28	5.63		
4.	Obedience					
	a) Private Aided	161	18.94	6.21	1.63	NS
	b) Private Unaided	170	20.11	6.78		
5.	Justice					
	a) Private Aided	161	17.72	5.38	0.79	NS
	b) Private Unaided	170	18.20	5.67		
II.	Total Moral Judgement					
	a) Private Aided	161	87.73	25.18	1.97	*
	b) Private Unaided	170	92.60	26.28		

* Significant at 0.05 level

NS = Not Significant

Table 4.25 indicates that the obtained t-value for the honesty dimension t = 2.28 is higher than the table value which is 1.97 significant at 0.05 level of significance. So the null hypothesis in this regard was rejected. The alternative hypothesis is formulated that there is significant difference in the honesty component of Moral Judgement of students studying in private aided and unaided schools. However the t values for the remaining 4 dimensions of Moral Judgement was found to be far below the table value and hence not significant. The null hypothesis in this regard has been accepted. The obtained t-value for total Moral Judgement t = 1.97 is above the table value which is 1.96. Therefore it is significant at 0.05 level. Therefore the null hypothesis in this regard was rejected. The alternative hypothesis is formulated namely there is significant difference in the total Moral Judgement of students studying in private aided and unaided schools. Students studying in private unaided type of management had higher mean score (92.60) than students studying in aided type of management.

Two-way Analysis of Variance

Major Hypothesis

22. There is no significant main and interaction effect of sex and type of management on the moral judgement of students.

Table 4.26

Summary of Analysis of Variance of Moral Judgement scores of students by sex and Type of Management.

Source of Variance	df	SS	MSS	F-value
Sex	1	3562.923	3562.923	5.913*
Type of Management	2	2358.101	1179.051	1.957 NS
Interaction	2	17753.557	8876.779	14.733**
Error	494	297646.599	602.523	
Total	499	321386.112	644.060	

** Significant at 0.01 level

* Significant at 0.05 level

NS = Not Significant

The analysis of variance of Moral Judgement of students by their sex and type of management indicated that the main effect of sex was significant as the obtained F value of sex (F = 5.913) was significant at 0.05 level. The null hypothesis in this regard was rejected. The obtained F value of type of management (F = 1.957) was not significant at 0.05 level. Therefore the null hypothesis was accepted. However, the interaction effect was significant at both the levels. The null hypothesis in this regard was rejected. This means that there is significant main effect of sex and interaction effect of sex and type of management on the Moral Judgement of students.

Major Hypothesis

23. There is no significant main and interaction effect of sex and parental behaviour on the moral judgement of students.

Table 4.27

Summary of Analysis of Variance of Moral Judgement scores of students by sex and Parental Behaviour.

Source of Variance	df	SS	MSS	F-value
Sex	1	7.993	7.993	.019 NS
Parental Behaviour	1	107716.198	107716.198	259.660 **
Interaction	1	4201.156	4201.156	10.127 **
Error	496	205758.552	414.836	
Total	499	321386.112	644.060	

** Significant at 0.01 level

* Significant at 0.05 level

NS = Not Significant

The analysis of variance of Moral Judgement of students by their sex and Parental Behaviour indicated that the main effect of sex was not affecting the Moral Judgement as the obtained F value of sex (F = 0.019) was not significant at both the levels. The main effect of parental behaviour was affecting the Moral Judgement as the obtained F value of parental behaviour (F = 259.660) was significant at both the levels. The null hypothesis in the first case was accepted and was rejected in the second case. However, the interaction effect (F = 10.127) was significant at both the levels. Therefore the null hypothesis was rejected. This means that there is significant main effect of parental behaviour and interaction effect of sex and Parental Behaviour on the Moral Judgement of students.

Major Hypothesis

24. There is no significant main and interaction effect of sex and father oriented child rearing practices on the moral judgement of students.

Table 4.28

Summary of Analysis of Variance of Moral Judgement scores of students by sex and Father oriented Child Rearing Practices.

Source of Variance	df	SS	MSS	F-value
Sex	1	1153.750	1153.750	2.386 NS
Father oriented Child Rearing Practices	1	76477.496	76477.496	158.158 **
Interaction	1	971.710	971.710	2.010 NS
Error	496	239841.036	483.550	
Total	499	321386.112	644.060	

** Significant at 0.01 level

* Significant at 0.05 level

NS = Not Significant

The analysis of variance of Moral Judgement of students by their sex and Father oriented Child Rearing Practices indicated that the main effect of sex was not affecting the Moral Judgement as the obtained F value of sex (F = 2.38) was not significant at both the levels. The main effect of Father oriented Child Rearing Practices was affecting the Moral Judgement as the obtained F value (F = 158.158) was significant at both the levels. The null hypothesis was rejected in this case. However the interaction effect was not significant at both 0.05 and 0.01 levels as the obtained F value was 2.010. The null hypothesis is accepted in this case. This means that there is significant main effect of Father oriented Child Rearing Practices on the Moral Judgement of students.

Major Hypothesis

25. There is no significant main and interaction effect of sex and mother oriented child rearing practices on the moral judgement of students.

Table 4.29

Summary of Analysis of Variance of Moral Judgement scores of students by sex and Mother oriented Child Rearing Practices.

Source of Variance	df	SS	MSS	F-value
Sex	1	775.776	775.776	1.527 NS
Mother oriented Child Rearing Practices	1	65601.008	65601.008	129.138 **
Interaction	1	91.671	91.671	0.180 NS
Error	496	251963.161	507.990	
Total	499	321386.112	644.060	

** Significant at 0.01 level

* Significant at 0.05 level

NS = Not Significant

The analysis of variance of Moral Judgement of students by their sex and Mother oriented Child Rearing Practices indicated that the main effect of sex (F = 1.52) and interaction effect (F = 0.180) was not significant at 0.05 level. The null hypothesis in this regard was accepted. However the main effect of Mother oriented Child Rearing Practices was affecting the Moral Judgement as the obtained F value was 129.138 was significant at both the levels. The null hypothesis was rejected. This means that there is significant main effect of Mother oriented Child Rearing Practices on the Moral Judgement of students.

Major Hypothesis

26. There is no significant main and interaction effect of sex and Emotional Maturity on the moral judgement of students.

Table 4.30

Summary of Analysis of Variance of Moral Judgement scores of students by sex and Emotional Maturity.

Source of Variance	df	SS	MSS	F-value
Sex	1	74.423	74.423	0.365 NS
Emotional Maturity	1	216658.420	216658.420	1062.828 **
Interaction	1	0.814	0.814	0.004 NS
Error	496	101110.079	203.851	
Total	499	321386.112	644.060	

** Significant at 0.01 level

* Significant at 0.05 level

NS = Not Significant

The analysis of variance of Moral Judgement of students by their sex and Emotional Maturity indicated that the main effect of sex and interaction effect (F = 0.365 and 0.004) were not significant at 0.05 level. The null hypotheses in this case was accepted. The main effect of Emotional Maturity (F = 1062.828) was significant at both 0.05 and 0.01 levels. The null hypothesis was rejected in this case. This means that there is significant main effect of Emotional Maturity on the Moral Judgement of students.

Major Hypothesis

27. There is no significant main and interaction effect of sex and personality traits on the moral judgement of students.

Table 4.31

Summary of Analysis of Variance of Moral Judgement scores of students by sex and Personality traits.

Source of Variance	df	SS	MSS	F-value
Sex	1	2654.864	2654.864	4.170 *
Personality traits	2	3167.453	3167.453	2.487 NS
Interaction	2	59.849	59.849	0.047 NS
Error	494	314541.940	636.725	
Total	499	321386.112	644.060	

** Significant at 0.01 level

* Significant at 0.05 level

NS = Not Significant

The analysis of variance of Moral Judgement of students by their sex and personality traits indicated that only the main effect of sex was affecting the Moral Judgement as the obtained F value of sex (F = 4.170) was significant at 0.05 level. However the main effect of personality traits and the interaction effect was not significant at 0.05 level. The null hypothesis was accepted in this case. This means that there is main effect of sex on the Moral Judgement of students.

Major Hypothesis

28. There is no significant main and interaction effect of sex and socio-economic status on the moral judgement of students.

Table 4.32

Summary of Analysis of Variance of Moral Judgement scores of students by sex and Socio-Economic Status.

Source of Variance	df	SS	MSS	F-value
Sex	1	3490.021	3490.021	5.450 *
Socio-Economic Status	1	77.732	77.732	0.121 NS
Interaction	1	152.581	152.581	0.238 NS
Error	496	317628.631	640.380	
Total	499	321386.112	644.060	

** Significant at 0.01 level * Significant at 0.05 level
NS = Not Significant

The analysis of variance of Moral Judgement of students by their sex and socio-economic status indicated that only the main effect of sex was affecting the Moral Judgement as the obtained F value of sex (F = 5.450) was significant at 0.05 level. The null hypothesis in this regard was rejected. But the main effect of socio-economic status and the interaction effect were not significant at 0.05 level. So the null hypothesis in this case was accepted. This means that there is significant main effect of sex on the Moral Judgement of students.

Major Hypothesis

29. There is no significant main and interaction effect of type of management and parental behaviour on the moral judgement of students.

Table 4.33

Summary of Analysis of Variance of Moral Judgement scores of students by Type of management and Parental Behaviour.

Source of Variance	df	SS	MSS	F-value
Type of management	2	1195.555	597.778	1.444 NS
Parental Behaviour	1	110329.914	110329.914	266.547 **
Interaction	2	4549.623	2274.811	5.496 **
Error	494	205758.552	414.836	
Total	499	321386.112	644.060	

** Significant at 0.01 level * Significant at 0.05 level
NS = Not Significant

The analysis of variance of Moral Judgement of students by type of management and Parental Behaviour indicated that the main effect of type of management was not affecting the Moral Judgement as the obtained F value (F = 1.444) was not significant at 0.05 level. The null hypothesis was accepted in this case. The main effect of parental behaviour and the interaction effect was significant at both 0.05 and 0.01 levels. The null hypothesis was rejected. This means that there is significant main effect of parental behaviour and interaction effect of type of management and Parental Behaviour on the Moral Judgement of students.

Major Hypothesis

30. There is no significant main and interaction effect of type of management and Father oriented child rearing practices on the moral judgement of students.

Table 4.34

Summary of Analysis of Variance of Moral Judgement scores of students by type of management and Father oriented Child Rearing Practices.

Source of Variance	df	SS	MSS	F-value
Type of management	2	4881.783	2440.891	5.144 **
Father oriented Child Rearing Practices	1	82227.955	82227.955	173.297 **
Interaction	2	2871.559	1435.780	3.026 *
Error	494	234399.182	474.492	
Total	499	321386.112	644.060	

** Significant at 0.01 level
* Significant at 0.05 level
NS = Not Significant

The analysis of variance of Moral Judgement of students by type of management and Father oriented Child Rearing Practices indicated that the main and interaction effect of type of management and Father oriented Child Rearing Practices were affecting the Moral Judgement as the obtained F value (F = 5.144, 173.297 and 3.026) was significant at both 0.05

and 0.01 levels. The null hypothesis in this regard were rejected. This means that there is significant main and interaction effect of type of management and Father oriented Child Rearing Practices on the Moral Judgement of students.

Major Hypothesis

31. There is no significant main and interaction effect of type of management and Mother oriented child rearing practices on the moral judgement of students.

Table 4.35

Summary of Analysis of Variance of Moral Judgement scores of students by type of management and Mother oriented Child Rearing Practices.

Source of Variance	df	SS	MSS	F-value
Type of management	2	4844.597	2422.299	4.866 **
Mother oriented Child Rearing Practices	1	71215.038	71215.038	143.050 **
Interaction	1	2118.885	1059.442	2.128 NS
Error	494	245928.912	497.832	
Total	499	321386.112	644.060	

** Significant at 0.01 level

* Significant at 0.05 level

NS = Not Significant

The analysis of variance of Moral Judgement of students by type of management and Mother oriented Child Rearing Practices indicated that the main effects were affecting the Moral Judgement as the obtained F values (4.866 and 143.050) were significant at 0.05 and 0.01 levels. The null hypotheses was rejected in this case. However the interaction effect (F = 2.128) was not significant at 0.05 level. The null hypothesis was accepted. This means that there is significant main effects of type of management and Mother oriented Child Rearing Practices on the Moral Judgement of students.

Major Hypothesis

32. There is no significant main and interaction effect of type of management and Emotional Maturity on the moral judgement of students.

Table 4.36

Summary of Analysis of Variance of Moral Judgement scores of students by type of management and Emotional Maturity.

Source of Variance	df	SS	MSS	F-value
Type of management	2	742.478	371.239	1.839 NS
Emotional Maturity	1	217744.948	217744.948	1078.586 **
Interaction	2	683.384	341.692	1.693 NS
Error	494	99728.713	201.880	
Total	499	321386.112	644.060	

** Significant at 0.01 level

* Significant at 0.05 level

NS = Not Significant

The analysis of variance of Moral Judgement of students by their type of management and Emotional Maturity indicated that only the main effect of Emotional Maturity was affecting the Moral Judgement as the obtained F value (F = 1078.586) was significant at both 0.05 and 0.01 levels. The null hypothesis was rejected in this case. However, the main effect of type of management and the interaction effect of type of management and Emotional Maturity was not affecting the Moral Judgement. This means that there is significant main effect of Emotional Maturity on the Moral Judgement of students.

Major Hypothesis

33. There is no significant main and interaction effect of type of management and personality traits on the moral judgement of students.

Table 4.37

Summary of Analysis of Variance of Moral Judgement scores of students by type of management and Personality traits.

Source of Variance	df	SS	MSS	F-value
Type of management	2	2586.731	1293.365	2.032 NS
Personality traits	2	2123.851	1061.926	1.669 NS
Interaction	4	3257.122	814.281	1.279 NS
Error	491	312486.392	636.428	
Total	499	321386.112	644.060	

** Significant at 0.01 level * Significant at 0.05 level
NS = Not Significant

The analysis of variance of Moral Judgement of students by their type of management and personality traits indicated that the main and the interaction effects of type of management and personality traits were not affecting the Moral Judgement as the obtained F value of type of management (F = 2.032), Personality traits (F = 1.66) and interaction (F = 1.27) were not significant at 0.05 level. The null hypothesis in this regard was accepted. This means that there is no significant main and interaction effects of type of management and personality traits on the Moral Judgement of students.

Major Hypothesis

34. There is no significant main and interaction effect of type of management and socio-economic status on the moral judgement of students.

Table 4.38

Summary of Analysis of Variance of Moral Judgement scores of students by type of management and socio-economic status.

Source of Variance	df	SS	MSS	F-value
Type of management	2	2595.414	1297.707	2.013 NS
Socio-Economic Status	1	70.435	70.435	0.109 NS

Interaction	2	318.811	159.406	0.247 NS
Error	494	318394.463	644.523	
Total	499	321386.112	644.060	

** Significant at 0.01 level * Significant at 0.05 level
NS = Not Significant

The analysis of variance of Moral Judgement of students by their type of management and socio-economic status indicated that both the main and interaction effects were not affecting the Moral Judgement as the obtained F values (2.013, 0.109 and 0.247) were not significant at 0.05 level. The null hypothesis in this case was accepted. This means that there is no significant main and interaction effect of type of management and socio-economic status on Moral Judgement of students.

Major Hypothesis

35. There is no significant main and interaction effect of parental behaviour and father oriented child rearing practices on the moral judgement of students.

Table 4.39

Summary of Analysis of Variance of Moral Judgement scores of students by parental behaviour and Father oriented Child Rearing Practices.

Source of Variance	df	SS	MSS	F-value
Parental behaviour	1	33706.429	33706.429	82.416 **
Father oriented Child Rearing Practices	1	6913.431	6913.431	16.904 **
Interaction	1	107.230	107.230	0.262 NS
Error	496	202852.515	408.977	
Total	499	321386.112	644.060	

** Significant at 0.01 level * Significant at 0.05 level

NS = Not Significant

The analysis of variance of Moral Judgement of students by their parental behaviour and Father oriented Child

Rearing Practices indicated that the main effect of both parental behaviour and father oriented child rearing practices were affecting the Moral Judgement as the obtained F values (82.416 and 16.904) were significant at both 0.05 and 0.01 levels. The null hypothesis was rejected in this case. However the interaction effect (F = 0.262) was not significant at both 0.05 and 0.01 levels. The null hypothesis was accepted. This means that there is main effect of Parental Behaviour and Father oriented Child Rearing Practices on the Moral Judgement of students.

Major Hypothesis

36. There is no significant main and interaction effect of parental behaviour and mother oriented child rearing practices on the moral judgement of students.

Table 4.40

Summary of Analysis of Variance of Moral Judgement scores of students by parental behaviour and Mother oriented Child Rearing Practices.

Source of Variance	df	SS	MSS	F-value
Parental behaviour	1	43872.719	43872.719	106.234 **
Mother oriented Child Rearing Practices	1	5118.801	5118.801	12.395 **
Interaction	1	156.711	156.711	0.379 NS
Error	496	204839.312	412.982	
Total	499	321386.112	644.060	

** Significant at 0.01 level

* Significant at 0.05 level

NS = Not Significant

The analysis of variance of Moral Judgement of students by their parental behaviour and Mother oriented Child Rearing Practices indicated that the main effect of both parental behaviour and mother oriented child rearing practices were affecting the Moral Judgement as the obtained F values (106.234 and 12.395) were significant at both 0.05 and 0.01 levels. The null hypothesis was rejected in this case. However the interaction effect was not significant at both 0.05 and 0.01 levels as the obtained F-value (0.379) was less than table values. The null hypothesis was accepted. This means that there is main effect of Parental Behaviour and Mother oriented Child Rearing Practices on the Moral Judgement of students.

Major Hypothesis

37. There is no significant main and interaction effect of parental behaviour and Emotional Maturity on the moral judgement of students.

Table 4.41

Summary of Analysis of Variance of Moral Judgement scores of students by parental behaviour and Emotional Maturity.

Source of Variance	df	SS	MSS	F-value
Parental behaviour	1	7910.787	7910.787	44.609 **
Emotional Maturity	1	121968.589	121968.589	687.780 **
Interaction	1	3244.693	3244.693	18.297 **
Error	496	87958.918	177.337	
Total	499	321386.112	644.060	

** Significant at 0.01 level

* Significant at 0.05 level

NS = Not Significant

The analysis of variance of Moral Judgement of students by their parental behaviour and Emotional Maturity revealed that both the main and interaction effects of parental behaviour and Emotional Maturity were affecting the Moral Judgement of students as the obtained F values (44.609, 687.780 and 18.297) were significant at 0.05 and 0.01 levels of significance. The null hypothesis in this regard was rejected. This means that there is significant main and interaction effects of parental behaviour and Emotional Maturity on the Moral Judgement of students.

Major Hypothesis

38. There is no significant main and interaction effect of parental behaviour and personality traits on the moral judgement of students.

Table 4.42

Summary of Analysis of Variance of Moral Judgement scores of students by parental behaviour and Personality traits.

Source of Variance	df	SS	MSS	F-value
Parental behaviour	1	81253.439	81253.439	197.337 **
Personality traits	2	4545.241	4545.241	5.519 **
Interaction	2	1609.660	804.830	1.955 NS
Error	494	203404.156	411.749	
Total	499	321386.112	644.060	

** Significant at 0.01 level

* Significant at 0.05 level

NS = Not Significant

The analysis of variance of Moral Judgement of students by their parental behaviour and personality traits indicated that the main effect of both were affecting the Moral Judgement as the obtained F values (197.337 and 5.519) were significant at 0.05 and 0.01 levels of significance. The null hypothesis was rejected. However the interaction effect was not significant at 0.05 and 0.01 levels of significance. The null hypothesis was accepted in this case. This means that there is main effect of parental behaviour and personality traits on the Moral Judgement of students.

Major Hypothesis

39. There is no significant main and interaction effect of parental behaviour and socio-economic status on the moral judgement of students.

Table 4.43

Summary of Analysis of Variance of Moral Judgement scores of students by parental behaviour and Socio-Economic Status.

Source of Variance	df	SS	MSS	F-value
Parental behaviour	1	111290.623	111290.623	262.917 **
Socio-Economic Status	1	10.930	10.930	0.026 NS
Interaction	1	.066	.066	0.000 NS
Error	496	209952.741	423.292	
Total	499	321386.112	644.060	

** Significant at 0.01 level

* Significant at 0.05 level

NS = Not Significant

The analysis of variance of Moral Judgement of students by their parental behaviour and socio-economic status indicated that only the main effect of parental behaviour was affecting the Moral Judgement as the obtained F value (F = 262.917) was significant at 0.05 and 0.01 levels of significance. The null hypothesis was rejected. The main effect of socio-economic status and the interaction effect were not significant at 0.05 and 0.01 levels of significance. Hence the null hypothesis was accepted. This means that there is significant main effect of parental behaviour on the Moral Judgement of students.

Major Hypothesis

40. There is no significant main and interaction effect of father oriented child rearing practices and mother oriented child rearing practices on the moral judgement of students.

Table 4.44

Summary of Analysis of Variance of Moral Judgement scores of students by Father oriented Child Rearing Practices and Mother oriented Child Rearing Practices.

Source of Variance	df	SS	MSS	F-value
Father oriented Child Rearing Practices	1	11953.337	11953.337	24.631 **
Mother oriented Child Rearing Practices	1	903.179	903.179	1.861 NS
Interaction	1	24.304	24.304	0.050 NS
Error	496	240707.895	485.298	
Total	499	321386.112	644.060	

** Significant at 0.01 level

* Significant at 0.05 level

NS = Not Significant

The analysis of variance of Moral Judgement of students by their Father oriented Child Rearing Practices and Mother oriented Child Rearing Practices indicated that only the main effect of Father oriented Child Rearing Practices was affecting the Moral Judgement as the obtained F value (F = 24.631) was significant at 0.05 and 0.01 levels of significance. The null hypothesis was rejected. The main effect of Mother oriented Child Rearing Practices and the interaction effect were not affecting the Moral Judgement as obtained F value (1.861 and 0.050) was not significant at 0.05 and 0.01 levels of significance. The null hypothesis was accepted. This means that there is main effect of Father oriented Child Rearing Practices on the Moral Judgement of students.

Major Hypothesis

41. There is no significant main and interaction effect of father oriented child rearing practices and Emotional Maturity on the moral judgement of students.

Table 4.45

Summary of Analysis of Variance of Moral Judgement scores of students by Father oriented Child Rearing Practices and Emotional Maturity.

Source of Variance	df	SS	MSS	F-value
Father oriented Child Rearing Practices	1	4865.131	4865.131	26.351 **
Emotional Maturity	1	145730.100	145730.100	789.332 **
Interaction	1	2243.794	2243.794	12.153 **
Error	496	91573.798	184.625	
Total	499	321386.112	644.060	

** Significant at 0.01 level
* Significant at 0.05 level
NS = Not Significant

The analysis of variance of Moral Judgement of students by their Father oriented Child Rearing Practices and Emotional Maturity indicated that both the main and interaction effects were affecting the Moral Judgement as the obtained F values (26.351, 789.332 and 12.153) were significant at both 0.05 and 0.01 levels. The null hypothesis was rejected. This means that there is significant main and interaction effects of Father oriented Child Rearing Practices and Emotional Maturity on the Moral Judgement of students.

Major Hypothesis

42. There is no significant main and interaction effect of father oriented child rearing practices and personality traits on the moral judgement of students.

Table 4.46

Summary of Analysis of Variance of Moral Judgement scores of students by Father oriented Child Rearing Practices and Personality traits.

Source of Variance	df	SS	MSS	F-value
Father oriented Child Rearing Practices	1	59693.807	59693.807	124.251 **
Personality traits	2	3826.838	1913.419	3.983 *
Interaction	2	837.068	418.534	0.871 NS
Error	494	237331.404	480.428	
Total	499	321386.112	644.060	

** Significant at 0.01 level
* Significant at 0.05 level
NS = Not Significant

The analysis of variance of Moral Judgement of students by their Father oriented Child Rearing Practices and personality traits indicated that the main effect of both Father oriented Child Rearing Practices and personality traits were affecting the Moral Judgement as the obtained F values (F = 124.251, 3.983) were significant at 0.05 and 0.01 levels of significance and 0.05 level respectively. The null hypothesis was rejected. However the interaction effect was not affecting the Moral Judgement scores as the obtained F-value (F = 0.871) was far below 0.05 level. The null hypothesis was accepted in this case. This means that there is significant main effect of Father oriented Child Rearing Practices and personality traits on the Moral Judgement of students.

Major Hypothesis

43. There is no significant main and interaction effect of father oriented child rearing practices and socio-economic status on the moral judgement of students.

Table 4.47

Summary of Analysis of Variance of Moral Judgement scores of students by Father oriented Child Rearing Practices and Socio-Economic Status.

Source of Variance	df	SS	MSS	F-value
Father oriented Child Rearing Practices	1	79096.865	79096.865	162.809 **
Socio-Economic Status	1	48.853	48.853	0.101 NS
Interaction	1	726.698	726.698	1.496 NS
Error	496	240970.402	485.827	
Total	499	321386.112	644.060	

** Significant at 0.01 level
* Significant at 0.05 level
NS = Not Significant

The analysis of variance of Moral Judgement of students by their Father oriented Child Rearing Practices and socio-economic status indicated that only the main effect of Father oriented Child Rearing Practices was affecting the Moral Judgement as the obtained F value (F = 162.809) was significant at 0.05 and 0.01 levels of significance. The null hypothesis was rejected. However, the main effect of socio-economic status and the interaction effect were not significant at 0.05 level of significance. Hence the null hypothesis was accepted. This means that there is main effect of Father oriented Child Rearing Practices on Moral Judgement of students.

Major Hypothesis

44. There is no significant main and interaction effect of mother oriented child rearing practices and Emotional Maturity on the moral judgement of students.

Table 4.48

Summary of Analysis of Variance of Moral Judgement scores of students by Mother oriented Child Rearing Practices and Emotional Maturity.

Source of Variance	df	SS	MSS	F-value
Mother oriented Child Rearing Practices	1	3964.297	3964.297	19.967 **
Emotional Maturity	1	156431.754	156431.754	829.747 **
Interaction	1	2148.744	2148.744	11.397 **
Error	496	93510.662	188.530	
Total	499	321386.112	644.060	

** Significant at 0.01 level

* Significant at 0.05 level

NS = Not Significant

The analysis of variance of Moral Judgement of students by their Mother oriented Child Rearing Practices and Emotional Maturity indicated that both the main and interaction effects were affecting the Moral Judgement as the obtained F values (19.967, 829.747 and 11.397) were significant at both 0.05 and 0.01 levels. The null hypothesis was rejected in this case. This means that there is significant main and interaction effects of Mother oriented Child Rearing Practices and Emotional Maturity on the Moral Judgement of students.

Major Hypothesis

45. There is no significant main and interaction effect of mother oriented child rearing practices and personality traits on the moral judgement of students.

Table 4.49

Summary of Analysis of Variance of Moral Judgement scores of students by Mother oriented Child Rearing Practices and Personality traits.

Source of Variance	df	SS	MSS	F-value
Mother oriented Child Rearing Practices	1	45916.064	45916.064	92.007 **
Personality traits	2	4100.450	2050.225	4.108 *
Interaction	2	2705.153	1352.576	2.710 NS
Error	494	246530.515	499.050	
Total	499	321386.112	644.060	

** Significant at 0.01 level

* Significant at 0.05 level

NS = Not Significant

The analysis of variance of Moral Judgement of students by their Mother oriented Child Rearing Practices and personality traits indicated that both the main effect was affecting the Moral Judgement as the obtained F = 92.007 significant at 0.05 and 0.01 levels of significance and F = 4.108 significant at 0.05 level respectively. The null hypothesis was rejected in this regard. The interaction effect was not significant at 0.05 and 0.01 levels of significance. The null hypothesis was accepted. This means that there is main effect of Mother oriented Child Rearing Practices and personality traits on the Moral Judgement of students.

Major Hypothesis

46. There is no significant main and interaction effect of mother oriented child rearing practices and socio-economic status on the moral judgement of students.

Table 4.50

Summary of Analysis of Variance of Moral Judgement scores of students by Mother oriented Child Rearing Practices and Socio-Economic Status.

Source of Variance	df	SS	MSS	F-value
Mother oriented Child Rearing Practices	1	68436.688	68436.688	134.496 **
Socio-Economic Status	1	170.651	170.651	0.335 NS
Interaction	1	267.581	267.581	0.526 NS
Error	496	252384.355	508.839	
Total	499	321386.112	644.060	

** Significant at 0.01 level

* Significant at 0.05 level

NS = Not Significant

The analysis of variance of Moral Judgement of students by their Mother oriented Child Rearing Practices and socio-economic status indicated that only the main effect of Mother oriented Child Rearing Practices was affecting the Moral Judgement as the obtained F value (F = 134.496) was significant at 0.05 and 0.01 levels of significance. The null hypothesis was rejected. However, the main effect of socio-economic status and the interaction effect was not significant at 0.05 and 0.01 levels of significance. Hence the null hypothesis was accepted. This means that there is main effect of Mother oriented Child Rearing Practices on Moral Judgement of students.

Major Hypothesis

47. There is no significant main and interaction effect of Emotional Maturity and personality traits on the moral judgement of students.

Table 4.51

Summary of Analysis of Variance of Moral Judgement scores of students by Emotional maturity and Personality traits.

Source of Variance	df	SS	MSS	F-value
Emotional maturity	1	175277.293	175277.293	860.448 **
Personality traits	2	454.824	227.412	1.116 NS
Interaction	2	88.006	44.003	0.216 NS
Error	494	100630.157	203.705	
Total	499	321386.112	644.060	

** Significant at 0.01 level

* Significant at 0.05 level

NS = Not Significant

The analysis of variance of Moral Judgement of students by their Emotional maturity and personality traits indicated that only the main effect of Emotional Maturity was affecting the Moral Judgement as the obtained F value (F = 860.448) was significant at 0.05 and 0.01 levels of significance. The null hypothesis was rejected. However, the main effect of personality traits and the interaction effect was not affecting the Moral Judgement as the obtained F values (1.116 and 0.216) were not significant at 0.05 and 0.01 levels of significance. The null hypothesis was rejected in this case. This means that there is significant main effect of Emotional maturity on the Moral Judgement of students.

Major Hypothesis

48. There is no significant main and interaction effect of Emotional Maturity and socio-economic status on the moral judgement of students.

Table 4.52

Summary of Analysis of Variance of Moral Judgement scores of students by Emotional maturity and Socio-Economic Status.

Source of Variance	df	SS	MSS	F-value
Emotional maturity	1	220099.095	220099.095	1079.055 **
Socio-Economic Status	1	0.420	0.420	0.964 NS
Interaction	1	13.367	13.367	0.664 NS
Error	496	101171.041	203.974	
Total	499	321386.112	644.060	

** Significant at 0.01 level

* Significant at 0.05 level

NS = Not Significant

The analysis of variance of Moral Judgement of students by their Emotional maturity and socio-economic status indicated that only the main effect of Emotional maturity was affecting the Moral Judgement as the obtained F value (F = 1079.055) was significant at 0.05 and 0.01 levels of significance. The null hypothesis was rejected. The main effect of socio-economic status and the interaction effect were not significant at 0.05 and 0.01 levels of significance. Hence the null hypothesis was accepted in this case. This means that there is main effect of Emotional Maturity on the Moral Judgement of students. It can be concluded that differences in emotional maturity and socio economic status accounted for significant difference in the Moral Judgement of students.

Major Hypothesis

49. There is no significant main and interaction effect of personality traits and socio-economic status on the moral judgement of students.

Table 4.53

Summary of Analysis of Variance of Moral Judgement scores of students by Personality traits and Socio-Economic Status.

Source of Variance	df	SS	MSS	F-value
Personality traits	2	4163.281	2081.640	3.243 *
Socio-Economic Status	1	486.764	486.764	0.758 NS
Interaction	2	208.710	104.335	0.163 NS
Error	494	317110.394	641.924	
Total	499	321386.112	644.060	

** Significant at 0.01 level

* Significant at 0.05 level

NS = Not Significant

The analysis of variance of Moral Judgement of students by their personality traits and socio-economic status indicated that only the main effect of personality traits was affecting the Moral Judgement as the obtained F value (F = 3.243) was significant at 0.05 level. The null hypothesis was rejected in this case. However, the main effect of socio economic status and the interaction effect were not significant at 0.05 and 0.01 levels of significance. Hence the null hypothesis was accepted in this regard. This means that there is significant main effect of personality traits on Moral Judgement of students. It can be concluded that differences in personality traits and socio-economic status accounted for significant difference in the Moral Judgement of students.

CHAPTER V

SUMMARY AND CONCLUSIONS

5.1 FINDINGS OF THE STUDY

The following findings are drawn after the analysis of the data:

1. There is a significant and positive correlation between all the dimensions of Moral Judgement of students namely, honesty, truthfulness, non-violence, obedience, justice and total moral judgement and their Parental Behaviour (r = 0.14, 0.12, 0.24, 0.15, 0.17 and 0.58).
2. There is a highly significant and positive correlation between all the dimensions of Moral Judgement of students namely, honesty, truthfulness, non-violence, obedience, justice and total moral judgement and their Father Child Rearing Practices (r = 0.64, 0.68, 0.16, 0.72, 0.52 and 0.64).
3. There is a highly significant and positive correlation between all the dimensions of Moral Judgement of students namely, honesty, truthfulness, non-violence, obedience, justice and total moral judgement and their Mother Child Rearing Practices (r = 0.65, 0.78, 0.72, 0.73, 0.70 and 0.54).
4. There is a highly significant and positive correlation between all the dimensions of Moral Judgement of students namely, honesty, truthfulness, non-violence,

obedience, justice and total moral judgement and their Emotional Maturity (r = 0.73, 0.51, 0.59, 0.68, 0.58 and 0.92).

5. There is a highly significant and positive correlation between all the dimensions of Moral Judgement of students namely, honesty, truthfulness, non-violence, obedience, justice and total moral judgement and their Personality Traits (Extroversion) (r = 0.63, 0.68, 0.61, 0.57, 0.62 and 0.71).
6. There is a highly significant and positive correlation between all the dimensions of Moral Judgement of students namely, honesty, truthfulness, non-violence, obedience, justice and total moral judgement and their Personality Traits (Introversion) (r = 0.52, 0.64, 0.59, 0.56, 0.67 and 0.71).
7. There is a highly significant and positive correlation between all the dimensions of Moral Judgement of students namely, honesty, truthfulness, non-violence, obedience, justice and total moral judgement and their Personality Traits (Ambiversion) (r = 0.46, 0.57, 0.63, 0.71, 0.52 and 0.67).
8. There is a significant difference in all the dimensions of moral judgement and total moral judgement of students as per differences in their Parental Behaviour. Students belonging to high Parental Behaviour group were having higher mean scores on all the dimensions of moral judgement, namely, honesty (20.96), truthfulness (19.08), non-violence (20.71), obedience (22.91) and justice (20.48) and total moral judgement (104.17) than the students belonging to low Parental Behaviour group [honesty (15.17), truthfulness (13.64), non-violence (14.85), obedience (15.75) and justice (14.88) dimensions and total moral judgement (74.31)].
9. There is a significant difference in all the dimensions of moral judgement and total moral judgement of students as per differences in their Father-oriented Child Rearing

Practices. Students belonging to high Father-oriented Child Rearing Practices group were having higher mean scores on all the dimensions of moral judgement, namely, honesty (20.18), truthfulness (18.36), non-violence (20.04), obedience (21.95) and justice (19.87) and total moral judgement (100.43) than the students belonging to low Father-oriented Child Rearing Practices group [honesty (15.37), truthfulness (13.81), non-violence (14.88), obedience (15.99) and justice (14.88) dimensions and total moral judgement (74.94)].

10. There is a significant difference in all the dimensions of moral judgement and total moral judgement of students as per differences in their Mother-oriented Child Rearing Practices. Students belonging to high Mother-oriented Child Rearing Practices group were having higher mean scores on all the dimensions of moral judgement, namely, honesty (20.06), truthfulness (18.34), non-violence (19.90), obedience (21.81) and justice (19.72) and total moral judgement (99.84) than the students belonging to low Mother-oriented Child Rearing Practices group [honesty (15.62), truthfulness (13.94), non-violence (15.19), obedience (16.30) and justice (15.19) dimensions and total moral judgement (76.26)].

11. There is a significant difference in all the dimensions of moral judgement and total moral judgement of students as per differences in their Self-Knowledge component of emotional maturity. Students belonging to high self-knowledge component emotional maturity were having higher mean scores on all the dimensions of moral judgement, namely, honesty (22.22), truthfulness (19.84), non-violence (22.10), obedience (24.77) and justice (22.09) and total moral judgement (111.05) than the students belonging to low Self-knowledge component of emotional maturity [honesty (15.18), truthfulness (13.94), non-violence (15.30), obedience

(16.20) and justice (15.15) dimensions and total moral judgement (76.72)].

12. There is a significant difference in all the dimensions of moral judgement and total moral judgement of students as per differences in their Acceptance of Reality component of emotional maturity. Students belonging to high acceptance of Reality component of emotional maturity were having higher mean scores on all the dimensions of moral judgement, namely, honesty (20.95), truthfulness (19.14), non-violence (20.95), obedience (22.8) and justice (20.69) and total moral judgement (104.60) than the students belonging to low Acceptance of Reality component of emotional maturity [honesty (14.58), truthfulness (13.01), non-violence (13.95), obedience (15.10) and justice (14.04) dimensions and total moral judgement (70.72)].
13. There is a significant difference in all the dimensions of moral judgement and total moral judgement of students as per differences in their Self-Control component of emotional maturity. Students belonging to high self-Control component emotional maturity were having higher mean scores on all the dimensions of moral judgement, namely, honesty (22.51), truthfulness (20.21), non-violence (22.24), obedience (24.90) and justice (22.49) and total moral judgement (112.36) than the students belonging to low Self-Control component of emotional maturity [honesty (14.69), truthfulness (13.45), non-violence (14.40), obedience (15.10) and justice (14.03) dimensions and total moral judgement (71.69)].
14. There is a significant difference in all the dimensions of moral judgement and total moral judgement of students as per differences in their Social adjustment component of emotional maturity. Students belonging to high social adjustment component emotional maturity were having higher mean scores on all the dimensions of moral

judgement, namely, honesty (22.57), truthfulness (20.24), non-violence (22.56), obedience (25.33) and justice (22.51) and total moral judgement (113.23) than the students belonging to low Social adjustment component of emotional maturity [honesty (15.54), truthfulness (14.20), non-violence (15.10), obedience (15.97) and justice (14.97) dimensions and total moral judgement (75.79)].

15. There is a significant difference in all the dimensions of moral judgement and total moral judgement of students as per differences in their Consistency component of emotional maturity. Students belonging to high Consistency component emotional maturity were having higher mean scores on all the dimensions of moral judgement, namely, honesty (21.51), truthfulness (19.55), non-violence (21.33), obedience (23.68) and justice (21.34) and total moral judgement (107.43) than the students belonging to low Consistency component of emotional maturity [honesty (13.80), truthfulness (12.41), non-violence (13.38), obedience (13.95) and justice (13.14) dimensions and total moral judgement (66.68)].

16. There is a significant difference in all the dimensions of moral judgement and total moral judgement of students as per differences in their Self-confidence component of emotional maturity. Students belonging to high self-confidence component emotional maturity were having higher mean scores on all the dimensions of moral judgement, namely, honesty (22.20), truthfulness (19.94), non-violence (22.05), obedience (24.87) and justice (22.10) and total moral judgement (111.17) than the students belonging to low Self-confidence component of emotional maturity [honesty (14.93), truthfulness (13.65), non-violence (14.54), obedience (15.13) and justice (14.33) dimensions and total moral judgement (72.60)].

17. There is a significant difference in all the dimensions of moral judgement and total moral judgement of students as per differences in emotional maturity. Students belonging to high emotional maturity were having higher mean scores on all the dimensions of moral judgement, namely, honesty (20.06), truthfulness (18.34), non-violence (19.90), obedience (21.81) and justice (19.72) and total moral judgement (99.84) than the students belonging to low emotional maturity [honesty (14.33), truthfulness (13.23), non-violence (14.10), obedience (14.70) and justice (13.76) dimensions and total moral judgement (70.13)].
18. There is no significant difference in the total Moral Judgement scores and all the dimensions of students as per differences in their Personality Traits. Ambivert students had higher mean scores on the total Moral Judgement (M = 95.17) than Extroverts (M = 87.10) and Introverts (M = 89.60).
19. There is no significant difference in the total moral judgement scores and all the dimensions of moral judgement of 10th standard students as per differences in their socio-economic status.
20. There is a significant difference in the total moral judgement scores and the honesty and truthfulness dimensions of boys and girls. Girls had higher mean scores on honesty (M = 17.26) and truthfulness (M = 18.91) components and the total Moral Judgement (M = 92.08) than boys [honesty (M = 17.29) and truthfulness (M = 17.29) components and the total Moral Judgement (M = 86.76)].
21. There is no significant difference in the total moral judgement scores of students studying in government and private aided schools.
22. There is a significant difference in the honesty dimension of moral judgement scores of students studying in

government and private unaided schools. Students studying in unaided schools had higher mean scores (18.92) than students studying in government schools (17.76).

23. There is a significant difference in the honesty dimensions and total moral judgement scores of students studying in private aided and unaided schools. Students studying in private unaided schools had higher mean scores (Honesty – 18.92 and Moral Judgement – 92.60) than students studying in private aided schools (Honesty – 17.59 and total Moral Judgement – 87.73).
24. The main effect of sex and interaction effect of sex and type of management on the moral judgement of students are significant at 0.05 and 0.01 levels.
25. The main effect of parental behaviour and interaction effect of sex and parental behaviour on the moral judgement of students are significant at 0.05 and 0.01 levels.
26. The main effect of father oriented child rearing practices on moral judgement of students is significant at 0.05 and 0.01 levels. But the main effect of sex on moral judgement of students and interaction effect of sex and father oriented child rearing practices are not significant.
27. The main effect of mother oriented child rearing practices on moral judgement of students is significant at 0.05 and 0.01 levels. But the main effect of sex on moral judgement of students and interaction effect of sex and mother oriented child rearing practices are not significant.
28. The main effect of emotional maturity on moral judgement of students is significant at 0.05 and 0.01 levels. But the main effect of sex on moral judgement of students and interaction effect of sex and emotional maturity are not significant.

29. The main effect of sex on moral judgement of students is significant at 0.05 level. But the main effect of personality traits on moral judgement of students and interaction effect of sex and personality traits are not significant.
30. The main effect of sex on moral judgement of students is significant at 0.05 level. But the main effect of socio-economic status on moral judgement of students and interaction effect of sex and socio-economic status are not significant.
31. The main effect of parental behaviour and the interaction effect of parental behaviour and type of management on the moral judgement of students are significant at 0.05 and 0.01 levels. However the main effect of type of management on moral judgement of students is not significant.
32. The main effect of type of management and father oriented child rearing practices on the moral judgement of students is significant at 0.05 and 0.01 levels. However the interaction effect is significant at 0.05 level.
33. The main effect of type of management and mother oriented child rearing practices on the moral judgement of students is significant at 0.05 and 0.01 levels.
34. The main effect of emotional maturity on the moral judgement of students is significant at 0.05 and 0.01 levels.
35. There is no significant main and interaction effects of type of management and personality traits on the moral judgement of students.
36. There is no significant main and interaction effects of type of management and socio-economic status on the moral judgement of students.
37. The main and interaction effects of parental behaviour and father oriented child rearing practices on the moral judgement of students are significant at 0.05 and 0.01 levels.

38. The main and interaction effects of parental behaviour and mother oriented child rearing practices on the moral judgement of students are significant at 0.05 and 0.01 levels.
39. The main and interaction effects of parental behaviour and emotional maturity on the moral judgement of students are significant at 0.05 and 0.01 levels.
40. The main and interaction effects of parental behaviour and personality traits on the Moral judgement of students are significant at 0.05 and 0.01 levels.
41. The main effect of parental behaviour on the moral judgement of students is significant at 0.05 and 0.01 levels. However the main effect of socio-economic status and the interaction effect of parental behaviour and socio-economic status are not significant.
42. The main effect of father oriented child rearing practices on the moral judgement of students is significant at 0.05 and 0.01 levels. However the main effect of mother oriented child rearing practices and the interaction effect of father oriented child rearing practices and mother oriented child rearing practices are not significant.
43. The main and interaction effects of father oriented child rearing practices and emotional maturity on the moral judgement of students are significant at 0.05 and 0.01 levels.
44. The main effect of father oriented child rearing practices on moral judgement of students is significant at 0.05 and 0.01 levels. But the main effect of personality traits on moral judgement of students is significant at 0.05 level. However the interaction effect is not significant.
45. The main effect of father oriented child rearing practices on the moral judgement of students is significant at 0.05 and 0.01 levels. However the main effect of socio-

economic status and the interaction effect of father oriented child rearing practices and socio-economic status are not significant.

46. The main and interaction effects of mother oriented child rearing practices and emotional maturity on the moral judgement of students are significant at 0.05 and 0.01 levels.
47. The main effect of mother oriented child rearing practices on the moral judgement of students is significant at 0.05 and 0.01 levels. But the main effect of personality traits on the moral judgement of 10th standard students is significant at 0.05 level. However the interaction effect is not significant.
48. The main effect of mother oriented child rearing practices on the moral judgement of students is significant at 0.05 and 0.01 levels. However the main effect of socio-economic status and the interaction effect of mother oriented child rearing practices and socio-economic status are not significant.
49. The main effect of emotional maturity on the moral judgement of students is significant at 0.05 and 0.01 levels. However the main effect of personality traits and the interaction effect of emotional maturity and personality traits are not significant.
50. The main effect of emotional maturity on the moral judgement of students is significant at 0.05 and 0.01 levels. However the main effect of socio-economic status and the interaction effect of emotional maturity and socio-economic status are not significant.
51. The main effect of personality traits on the moral judgement of students is significant at 0.05 level. However the main effect of socio-economic status and the interaction effect of personality traits and socio-economic status are not significant.

5.2 LIMITATIONS OF THE STUDY

1. The study is limited to students in the City of Bangalore. There were as many as 924 secondary schools in the City of Bangalore at the time of data collection, out of which only 20 schools have been selected. Though Bangalore is an urban area, of late the growth of Bangalore City is phenomenal because many people are migrating from rural areas as well are added to the population of Bangalore. Thus, the limitation that the study is confined to an urban area may not be limitation in the true sense when considered from this point of view.
2. The investigator has selected only students as sample for the research study. This has been done due to the implicit limitations that have been there in the study from the point of view of cost and effort.
3. The researcher could include only a few independent variables in the present study. This has been purposefully done to do an indepth analysis of these variables.

5.3 EDUCATIONAL IMPLICATIONS

The following educational implications have been drawn from the findings of the study.

To educate a man in mind and not in morals is to educate a menace to society.

1) The primary function of the family is to give the child an insight into the culture that it has inherited. If parents follow a code of conduct they will be setting a good example for children to imbibe the spirit of culture. This would help the child in developing the desirable qualities of moral behaviour. The responsibility for character development and value formation lies within the family. Therefore parents have to be role models for their children. Parental counselling should be provided by schools. When schools work together with

families to support learning, children are inclined to succeed not just in school but throughout their life.

2) The study revealed that child rearing practices adopted by parents has a significant impact on the moral judgement of students. It is therefore very necessary on the part of parents to adopt appropriate child rearing practices. Too much of authoritarianism or too much of permissiveness is harmful especially during adolescence. Parents have to be cautious as to when they have to be authoritative and in what matters they can be lenient.

3) For the students to attain higher levels of emotional maturity that help them to certain make meaningful moral judgement, enough opportunity for self expression in home and schools should be provided. Parents must talk to their children and sort it out when they have any moral problems. Children must be given an opportunity for their feelings, clarification and discussions on moral issues.

4) Personality development programmes should be arranged in the schools. Each child is unique. Every child at home and at school must be treated according to his abilities and capabilities. Comparison of two children should be avoided. Children must be given freedom with proper discipline.

5) Role of teacher is very significant in cultivating moral, social and spiritual values in children. The ideal personality of the teacher is very much influential on moral development of the students. Teacher is considered as friend, philosopher and guide. So teacher's personal activities and behaviours have tremendous bearing on students. That is why, the teacher should establish and maintain clear standards of behaviour and encourage his pupils to behave towards himself, towards one another and towards the entire community in a desirable way. Most of the

practical programmes suggested for inculcation of social, moral and spiritual values in children depend on the sincerity and resourcefulness of teacher in the process of implementation. Therefore, the duty of the teacher is to see that all activities and programmes are undertaken in true spirit and directed towards the goal. Teacher is a model to the pupil. In past the teacher was regarded as preceptor, the pupil as disciple. Teacher, through his nobles activities and exemplary services influenced the personality of the child. Teacher's personality should be ideal to make the child pay him utmost reverence. Teacher is the embodiment of Brahma, Vishnu and Maheshwar.

6) The teacher can make use of direct and indirect methods of moral instruction which may include, stories, epic episodes, illustrations from the biographies of great personalities of the world, materials drawn from the great sources of the world literature, pointing out at the living personalities, from history, fables and fairy-tales, one can draw from any known materials. This should be supplemented with authoritarian injunctions, indoctrinations, physical and mental disciplines, and the actual opportunities for the child to practise the moral values in his own life. Moral behaviour to be internalised by the child should go through the process of (i) knowledge about it; (ii) emotional overtones associated with it; (iii) development of it into a habit; (iv) transforming itself into a psychological disposition; (v) becoming a permanent trait of the personality.

7) The students may be encouraged to read and prepare their own presentations about the moral precepts they have gathered, and symposiums may be organised to help them discuss their own views without the adult interference. The teachers should only organise them and leave it to children to run it by themselves. The process of internalisation of moral values by the

children must be smooth, soft, and natural and at no time force, either physical or mental should be used. This would only spoil the whole effort. After all in the ultimate analysis it is child who takes a decision to be virtuous and moral rather than the teacher who cannot take any decision on his (child's) behalf. If we remember that we do not want to turn our child into a moral robot, without his own sense of discrimination and autonomy, then we should provide an opportunity for the child to examine his internalised concepts, and become conscious of them within himself, by allowing him to bring it to his conscious and rational faculty, and allowing him to modify his ideas in the light of his own understanding. This is a difficult task because each child would get his/her own doubts as he studies them in the background of his social realities. It is here that the role of the teacher becomes very significant. One can always snub an enquiring child to keep quiet, if he (the teacher) does not know the answer, or does not have the patience to answer the questions of the child.

8) In the process of inculcation of democratic, social, moral and spiritual values in education, the role of the teacher can not be neglected at all. Thus, the teacher through different activities like instruction, rapport and organisation of curricular and co-curricular activities will be able to instill value-consciousness in children.

9) It would be very desirable, as suggested by the University Education Commission, to start work every day in all educational institutions with a few minutes of silent meditation either in the classroom or in a common hall. There could be some sort of prayer also which need not be addressed to any deity or ask for any favour, but which may be in the nature of an exhortation for self-discipline and devotion to some ideal. Occasionally, in these Assembly meetings, inspiring passages from great literature, religious as well

as secular, and pertaining to all important religions and cultures of the world, could be read with profit. Community singing of inspiring songs and hymns can be most effective at school stage.

10) One hour a week should be assigned to moral instruction. The teacher should encourage the habit of discussion in the class. Apart from this regular class instruction, suitable speakers may be invited to address the students on moral and spiritual values. Celebrations may be organised on the occasion of important festivals of all religions. Knowledge and appreciation of religions other than one's own and respect for their founders should be encouraged in various ways including essay competitions and impromptu speech.

11) Organised social service during holidays and outside class hours should be an essential part of extra-curricular activities. Such service should teach the dignity of manual labour, love of humanity, patriotism and self-discipline. Participation in games and sports should be compulsory and physical education, including sex hygiene, should be a normal part of school programme. Qualities of character and behaviour of students should form an essential part of the overall assessment of a student's performance at school.

12) Education should be man-making, and character building, bringing out young men and women of character, adhering to and following time-tested values of life. They have to equip themselves with moral values to overcome the evils which have cropped up in our society. Discipline, patriotism, honesty and hard work should be the lode-stars. We should be a forward nation for others to emulate. Let India arise, awake and march forward answering the call made by Swami Vivekananda.

5.4 SUGGESTIONS FOR FURTHER RESEARCH

1. A comparative study of the moral judgement of urban and rural students can be undertaken.
2. The impact of significant variables such as intelligence, values and religion on moral judgement of students can be attempted.
3. Cross-cultural studies on moral judgement of adolescents and the influence of cultural factors can be studied.
4. The influence of attitudes and beliefs on moral judgement of children can be investigated.
5. A study of the variations in the development of moral judgement of primary, middle and high school student in relation to school climate can be undertaken.

BIBLIOGRAPHY

1. Agarwal, R. (1985), "Study of feeling of security in morally developed and underdeveloped adolescents as related to their self concept and personality", *DAI*, November, Vol. 40, No. 5, p. 1882-A.
2. Andersop J.P., (1940), "The Relationships between certain aspects of parental behaviour and attitudes of Junior High School Pupils", New York Teacher College, Columbia University.
3. Andry, R.G. (1957), Faulty Paternal and Maternal Child Relationship, Affection and Delinquency, *British Journal of Delinquency*, 8; 34-48.
4. Anette Guldhammer B., "Factors in the college experience relating to moral judgement development", *DAI*, Vol. 43, January, p. 2250-A.
5. Armentrout, J.A. (1972), "Sociometric classroom popularity and children's reports of parental child rearing behaviours", *Journal of Clinical Psychology*, 31, 444-48.
6. Aronfreed (1960), "Internal and External Orientation in the Moral Behaviour of Children: The Relevance of the Child's Position in Society and of Maternal Disciplinary Measures", paper to Amer. Psych. Assoc., Ohio, (1960).
7. Aroundekar, K., *Case Studies of Child Rearing Practices of 10 Families from Higher and Lower Socio-Economic*

Group, Unpublished M.Sc. Thesis, Child Development Department, Faculty of Home Science, M.S. University, Baroda, (1965).

8. Bandura, A. and McDonald, F.J. (1963), "The Influence of Social Reinforcement and the Behaviour of Models in Shaping Children's Moral Judgements", *F. Abnor. and Society. Psych.*, 67, 3, 274-81.
9. Baumol, W.J. Economic Theory and Operations Analysis, Prentice Hall of India.
10. Benninga Jacques, "The relationship of self concept, sex and intelligence to moral judgement in young children", *Dissertation Abstracts International*, April (1977), Vol. 37, No. 10, p. 6357-A.
11. Beriman, M. (1940), Why boys and girls leave school, *Am. Teach.* 33, 20.
12. Bhargava (1986), "A Study of Moral Judgement among children at concrete and formal operational stages and its relationship with the variable of Home and Educational Environment", *DAI*, May, Vol. 51, No. 10, p. 6231-A.
13. Bhushan, L.T. (1970), *Manual for Religiosity Scale*, National Psychological Corporation, Agra,.
14. Bindu Parikh (1969), "Study on development of Moral Judgement and its relation to Family Environmental Factors in Indian and American Families", *DAI*, April, Vol. 42, No.3, p. 1233-A.
15. Bostrom, C. (1981), "Family interaction and the child's ego functions", *Psychological Abstracts*, 68, 884.
16. Bowlby, J. (1953), *Child Care and Growth of Love*, England.
17. Bridge, K.M. (1920), "A Genetic Theory of Emotions", *J. Genetic Psychol*, 37 : 514-27.
18. Bull J. Norman (1969), *Moral Education*, Routledge and Kegan Paul Limited, London.

19. Bull J. Norman (1969), *Moral Judgement from Childhood to Adolescence,* Routledge and Kegan Paul, London.
20. Burgers, E.W. (1947), The Family and Sociological Research, Social Force, 26, Oct., pp. 1-19.
21. Burton, P.W. (1946), Newspaper reading behaviour of high school students, *Sch. & Soc.*, 63, 86.
22. Bush James Dean (1982), A Comparison of the effect of Kohlberg's Dilemmas vs. Alerate Dilemma in the Moral stating of Adolescents, *DAI,* June, Vol. 42, No. 12, p. 5010-A.
23. C.L. Kundu (1977), *Personality Development A Critique of Indian Studies,* Vishal Publications, Kurukshetra.
24. Chauhan, N.S. & Tiwari, G.P. (1969), *Early Dropouts: Two hypotheses, Indian Education,* Vol. VIII, No. 5 & 6, Agra (India).
25. Chauhan, N.S. (1968), *Truancy among School Going Boys,* (Ph.D. Thesis), (1963), Sri Ram Mehra & Co., Agra.
26. Chauhan, N.S. Tiwari, G.P. & Gupta R.P. (1968-69), "Dropout Behaviour as function of Family Treatment", *A Res. Journal of Education Psychology,* Vol. II, No. 4, 5, 6, pp. 163-167.
27. Chong, D.C.K. (1982), "A study of the self-esteem of delinquent male adolescents and the perceived degree of their parents' child rearing practices", *Dissertation Abstracts International,* 42, 4360-A.
28. Chopra, O.P. *Tax Ethics, Unaccounted Income or Black Money – the Norm of the Day,* Inter-India Publishing Company, (1985).
29. Clark, W.H., "Religion in Adolescence and Youth", *The Psychology of Religion,* The Macmillan and Company, New York, (1958).

30. Convey Stephen (1978), "Study on effects of human relations training on the Social, Emotional and Moral Development of Students", *DAI*, November, Vol. 22, No. 4, p. 3314-A.

31. Cowan, D.B. (1982), "Mother custody versus joint custody: Children's parental relationships and adjustment", *Dissertation Abstracts International*, 43, 726-A.

32. Cox Edwin, *Changing Aims in Religious Education*, Routledge and Kegam Paul Ltd., New York.

33. Cyert, R.M. and J.G. March (1956), "Organisational Factors in the Theory of Oligopoly", *Quarterly Journal of Economics*, 70, pp.44-46.

34. David J. DePalma and Jeanne M. Foley (eds.) (1975), *Moral Development: Current Theory and Research*, Lawrence Erlbaum Associates, New Jersey.

35. Desai, M. (1966), "A Study of Child Rearing Practices in Tusoue Socio-economic Group", Unpublished M.Sc. Thesis, M S University, Baroda.

36. Devi, N R, *Child Rearing Practices in Rural Families at Two Income Levels*.

37. Dockstander (1979), "Comparative Study of Development Sex Differences in Moral Reasoning", *DAI*, Sept., Vol. 40, No.3, p.1239 A.

38. Dolores, Landen Mekeller, "A study of two methods of training upon the development of moral judgement in young children," *DAI*, Vol.37, February, P 4828-A.

39. Dossard, James, H.S. et al. (1955), Personality roles in the large family, Child Development, pp. 71-78.

40. Downey, Meriel and Kelly A.V. (1978), *Moral Education Theory and Practice*, Harper and Row Publishers, London.

41. Durkheim, Emile (1961), Moral Education, The free press of Glenior Inc, New York,.

42. Durkin, D. (1959), "Children's Concepts of Justice: A Comparison with the Piaget Data", *Child Development*, 30, 59-67.

43. Elizabeth Hurlock (1955), *Adolescent Development*, 2nd Edition, McGraw Hill Book Company Pvt. Ltd.

44. English, H.B. (1929), "The Cases of the Conditioned Fear Response", *Abnormal, Society. Psychol.* 25 : 221-275.

45. Erkison, H. *Childhood Society.*

46. Evans Charles Samuel (1981), "Relationship of stages of Moral Development to Knowledge of Kohlberg's Theory of Moral Development in High School Students", *DAI*, August, Vol. 42, No. 2, p. 648-A.

47. Faizunsia and Pharmeshwaran, E.G. (1965 & 1968), "Maternal Behaviour and Behaviour Problems in Children", *Research Bulletin*, Department of Psychology, Osmania University (I) 46-55,.

48. Fefis Daniel Francis (1978), The relationship of predictive ability, empathy, intelligence and sex to moral judgement in adolescents, *DAI*, June, Vol. 39, No. 2, p. 7161-A.

49. Fullerton, D, A T. King, B.T. Shoven and J. Walley (1981), "Tax Integration in the U.S. A. General Equilibrium Approach", *American Economic Review*, 71, pp.667-691.

50. Fullerton, D, B.T. Shoven and J. Walley, "General Equilibrium Analysis of the U.S. Taxation Policy in the Treasury Department – Compendium of Tax Research", U S Government Printing Office.

51. Fullerton, D, B.T. Shoven and J. Walley, "Replacing the U.S. Income Tax with a Progressive Consumption Tax – A Sequenced General Equilibrium Approach", IER.

52. Gargiulo, Richards MESKK and Jamet Sulick A, "Moral Judgement in Retardes and Non-retardes School age children", *The Journal of Psychology*, Vol. 99, May, p. 23.

53. Garrett and Woodworth (1966), *Statistics in Psychology and Education*, Vakils Feffer and Simons Ltd., Bombay.

54. Garrett, H.E. (1973), *Statistics in Psychology and Education*, Seventh Indian Reprint, Bombay: Vakils, Feffer and Simons Private Ltd., pp.416-451.

55. Gessel, A and Thompson, H. (1941), "Twins T and G from Infancy of Adolescene: A biogenic study of Individual differences by the method of cotwin control", *Genetic Psychology Monograph*, 24 : 3-12.

56. Glueck, S. and Glueck, E. (1950), *Unravelling Juvenile Delinquency*, Massachusettes: Harvard University Press, Cambridge.

57. Gongre Willie Marvin (1981), "A Study of Moral Judgement using the defining issues test for three ethnic group at Bacone College, *DAI*, Nov., Vol. 42, No. 5, p. 1986-A.

58. Goodenough, F.L. (1931), "Anger in your Children", University of Minnesota, Minneapolis and Expression of Emotions in a Blind-deaf Child. *J. of Abnormal Inc. Pschol*, 27 :" 328-333.

59. Gopalaiah, G., "A Study of Moral Judgement in children experiments in Education", *Indian Psychological Abstracts*, Vol. 30, No. 1, March, p. 297.

60. Gorman Teresa Patriva (1979), *A Study of Moral Judgement and Religious Knowledge Scores of Catholic High School Boys from Catholic Public School.*

61. Gupta, A.K. (1987), *Parental Influences on Adolescents*, Ariana Publishing House, New Delhi.

62. Harris, C.W. (ed.), Harris, C.W. (ed.) (1960), *Encyclopedia of Educational Research*, 3rd ed., The Macmillan Company, New York.

63. Hilton James Michael (1978), "The relationship between the level of Moral Judgement of High School Students and their levels of Interpersonal Trust, Socio-Economic Status and Intelligence", *DAI*, December, Vol. 39, No. 6, p. 3375-A.

64. Irani, J. *Pattern of Childcare in 50 Middle Class Parsi Families in an Industrial Urban Community.*

65. Irwin, G. Sarason (1972), *Personality: An Objective Approach*, 2nd edn., John Wiley & Sons, Inc., New York.

66. Irwin, O.C. (1932), "Infant Responses to Vertical Movements", *Child Development*, 3 (167016).

67. Issacs, Susan (1932), *Social Development in Young Children: a Study of Beginnings*, Humanities Press Inc., New York.

68. Jersild, A.J. (1957), *Child Psychology*, Longon Staples Press.

69. Johnson Maris Barnes (1981), "A Study to determine the effect of moral development among sixth grade students utilizing Kohlberg's Theory of Moral Development and selected children stories", *DAI*, December, Vol. 42, No. 6, p. 2472-a.

70. Johnson, R.C. and Medinnus, G.R. (1964), *Child Psychology: Behaviour and Development*, John Wiley and Sons, New York.

71. Johnston Mary Anne (1980), "Relationship between Moral Judgement and Moral Behaviour Studies of Fifth Grade students in dissimilar setting", *DAI*, June, Vol. 40, No. 12, p. 6202-A.

72. Jones, H E and Jones, M L. "The Galvanic skin reflex as related to overt Emotional Repression", *Amer. J. Psychol*, 4 : 4 : 241-251.

73. Jones, H E and Jones, M L. (1935), "The Galvanic skin reflex in infancy", *Child Development*, 1, 106-110.

74. Kakkar, S.B. (1970), "Family Conflicts in Scholastic Achievement", *Indian Journal of Psychology*, 45, 159-165.

75. Kay, William (1970), *Moral Development*, George Allen and Unwin Ltd., London.

76. Kenvin Willard, A. (1981), "A Study of the Effect of Systematic Value Instruction on Level of Moral Judgement", *DAI*, October, Vol. 42, No. 4, p. 1582-A.

77. Khan, S, *Patterns of Child Rearing of 50 Middle Class Muslim Families in an Industrial Urban community.*

78. Kipust Philip Joseph (1984), "Moral Development and Self Concept of Adolescent Boys and Girls", *DAI*, May, Vol. 44, No. 11, p. 3327-A.

79. Koch, H.L. (1955), "Relations of certain family constellation: Characteristics and the attitudes of children towards adult", *Child Development*, 26, pp. 13-40.

80. Lady Irwin College, (1977), Child Upbringing practices in a Community Development Block, Delhi State.

81. Lehner, G.F.J. & Kube, E. (1955), *The Dynamics of Personal Adjustment*, N.J. Prentice Hall Inc.

82. Lewis Christing Lynne (1982), "The relationship of moral development and cognitive development within gifted students examined in the light of variables of sex, socio-economic status and age", *DAI*, June, Vol. 42, No. 12, Part I, p. 5088 A.

83. Lickona, Thomas (ed.) (1960), *Moral Development and Behaviour*, Philosophical Library, New York.

84. Madan, T.N. (1965), *Family and Kinship*, Asia Publishing House, Bombay.

85. Madhok, R. *Child Rearing Practices Among rural Women of Mahipalpur*, New Delhi.

86. Majumdar, D.N. (1962), *Caste and Communication in an Indian Village*, Asia Publishing House, Bombay.

87. Mandelbaum, F.G. (1970), *Villages, Family and Jati*, Popular Prakashan, Bombay.

88. Manjuvani (2000), *Influence of Home and School Environment on Mental Health of Children*, Discovery Publishing House, New Delhi.

89. Mark, Joseph, C. (1953), "The Attitude of Mothers of Male Schizophrenic toward Child Behaviour", *Journal Abn. Psychology*, 48, pp. 185-189.

90. Martin, A.R. (1943), "A Study of Parental Attitudes and their influence upon Personality Development", *Education*, 596-608.

91. Mast, Cruce, "The Interrelationship of Critical Thinking, Empathy and Social Interest with Moral Judgement", *DAI*, Vol. 36, June, p. 2945-A.

92. Mathur S and Shah, I. (1963), "Mothers Attitude Towards Child Rearing Practices in Two Cultures", *Indian Journal of Family Welfare*, Vol.X.

93. Michael Weston (1975), *Morality and the Self*, Basil Blackwell, Oxford.

94. Minturan, L, (1966), *Rajputs of Khalapur*, John Wiley, New York.

95. Mohundro Lauren Whitson (1977), "Stages of Moral Reasoning and Value Hierarchies of Sixth Grade Students", *DAI*, February, Vol. 37, No. 8, p. 5026-A.

96. Morris, Carstairs, G. (1968), *The Twice Born*, London.

97. Muralidharan (1969), "Size of Family and its relationship with the behaviour difficulties of Children", *Journal of Psychological Researches*, 13, 2, 94-100.

98. Murphy, G. (1953), *In the Minds of Men*, Basic Book Inc., New York.

99. Muthayya, B.C. (1972), *Child Welfare*, National Institute of Community Development, Hyderabad.

100. Nagarathna, B, "A Study of the Emotional Life of Children with special response to fear, anger and laughter", Master's Thesis, University of Mysore, Mysore.

101. National Council of Applied Economic Research (1969), "Long Term Projections for Iron and Steel".

102. National Council of Applied Economic Research, "Demand for Dalda".

103. National Council of Education Research and Training (1971), Report of the Education Commission 1964-66, "Education and National Development", New Delhi.

104. Nihira, K. Yusin, A. and Sinay, R. (1975), "Perception of Parental Behaviour by Adolescents in Crisis", *Psychological Reports*, 37, 787-93.

105. Nunn, G.D. (1983), "The psychological adjustment of youth as a function of family structure, family process, gender and development level", *Dissertation Abstracts International*, 43, 3272-A.

106. Patridge, E.A. (1939), *Social Psychology of Adolescence*, Prentice Hall, New York.

107. Pavlov, I.P. (1927), *Conditioned Refiexes*, Oxford University Press.

108. Piaget, Jean (1965), *The Moral Development of the Child*, Routledge and Regan Paul Ltd., New York.

109. Prasad and Prasad (1975), "Social and Emotional Development of Pre-School Children of Employed Mothers", *Journal of Social and Economic Studies*, 3 (1), 73-87,.

110. Pratt, K.L. Nelson, A.K. and Sun, M. (1930), "The Behaviour of New Born Infants", *Ohio State University Study Contr. Psychol.* No.10.

111. Punekar, V.B. (1959), *Son-Colis of Bombay*, Popular Book Depot, Bombay.

112. Rama Rao, K. (1986), *Moral Education: A Practical Approach*, Ramakrishna Institute of Moral and Spiritual Education, Mysore.

113. Rank, O. (1932), *Modern Education: A Critique of its Fundamental Ideas*, Alfred A. Knopf Inc., New York.

114. Rani, Urmila (1991), "Personal and Educational Environmental factors as correlates of moral judgement among urban and rural senior secondary students", Ph.D., Education, Punjab University, *Fifth Survey of Educational Research*.

115. Rao, G. and Sen, A. (1978), "Some psycho social aspects of juvenile delinquency", *Indian Journal of Clinical Psychology*, 60, 51-61.

116. Rao, M.L. and Mehta, P. (1979), "Communal canker in education: A comparative study of school and family environment", *Indian Educational Review*, 14, 75-87.

117. Reud, S. (1936), *The Problem of Anxiety*, W.W. Norton and Co., New York.

118. Roy Burman, B.K. (1961), *Village Survey Monograph*, Course of India.

119. Rutkowski, K.A. (1979), "The relationship between adolescent alienation and the adolescents' perception of early parent-child relationships", *Dissertation Abstracts International*, 40, 1970-A.

120. Sabapathy, Tara (1986), "A Study of the Relationship of Manifest Anxiety, Emotional Maturity and Social Maturity of X Standard Students to their Academic Achievement", Unpublished Ph.D. Thesis, Bangalore University, Bangalore.

121. Sachar, G.K. (1959), "Pattern of Child Rearing in 50 Middle Class Punjabi, Sikh Families", Unpublished Thesis, Tata Institute of Social Sciences, Bombay.

122. Scarf, H.E. and J.B. Shoven (ed.) (1984), *Applied General Equilibrium Analysis*, Cambridge University Press.

123. Schnurer Greeta (1977), "Sex differences and personality variables in the Moral Reasoning of young adults", *DAI*, January, Vol. 37, No. 7, p. 4244-A.

124. Sears, R.R. & Others (1957), *Pattern of Child Rearing*, Rown & Lerson, New York.

125. Seitz, W., Wehner, E.G. and Henke, M. (1970), "The relationship between parental style of education and personality characteristics of seven to eight year old boys", *Psychological Abstracts*, 45, 875.

126. Sethi, S. (1967), "A Study of Child Rearing Practices with reference to Feeding and Toilet Training in Two Villages", M.S. University, Baroda.

127. Sharma, S.R. (1999), *Moral and Values in Education*, Cosmo Publications, India.

128. Sherman, M. (1927-1928), "The differentiation of emotional responses in infants", *Journal of Coup Psychol.* 7 : 8.

129. Siefring John Joseph (1981), "Intelligence, Sex and Behavioural Correlates of Moral Reasoning of Public Junior High School Students", *DAI*, October, Vol. 42, No. 4, p.1560-A.

130. Smart, M.S. and Smart, R.G. (1966), *Living and Learning with Children*, Pston, Houghton Mittle.

131. Stevens, D.C., (1983), "A Study of the parental attitude and behaviour antecedents of child personality; Implication for parent education", *Dissertation Abstracts International*, 43, 3256-A.

132. Stollenberger, R.T. (1969), "Chinese American child raring practices and juvenile delinquency", *Child and Family*, 8, 279-88.

133. Symonds, M.A. (1939), "A Study of Parental Acceptance and Rejection", *American Journal of Orthopsychiatry*, 8, 679-88.

134. Thorpe, L.P. and Clark, W.W. (1959), *Manual for Mental Health Analysis*, California Test Bureau, Los Angeles.

135. Tiedemann, J., Langer, M., Schmidt, R. and Timn, T. (1981), "Social emotional student behaviour and parental rearing patterns", *Psychological Abstracts*, 68, 233.

136. Tiwari, G.P. (1971), *Family Dynamics of Dropouts at the Primary Level*, unpublished Ph.D. Thesis, Agra University, Agra.

137. Toai Ton (1978), "Adult Authority Figure, Grade, Sex and Moral Judgement in Vietnamese Immigrant Children, *DAI*, October, Vol. 39, No. 4, p. 2584-A.

138. Tripathi, Devendra K.M. and Girishwar Mishra, "Development of Moral Judgement in Indian Children", *Indian Psychological Abstracts*, Vol. 18, No. 1, p. 193.

139. Wallace G. & A.D.M. Walker (ed.) (1970), *The Definition of Morality*, Matheun & Co. Ltd, London.

140. Washburn, R.W. (1929), "A Study of Smiling and laughing infants in the year of life", *Genetic Psychol Monogr.* 6 : 39-531.

141. Watson, G. (1957), "Some personality differences in children related to strict or permissive parental discipline", *The Journal of Psychology*, 44, 227-49.

142. Watson, J.B. (1919), *Psychologist from the standpoint of a behaviorist*, J B Lippmidt Co., Philadelphia.

143. Wright and Derek, "A Study of the Relationship between Moral Judgement and Religious Belief in a Sample of English Adolescents", *The Journal of Social Psychology*, Vol. 72, p. 135-144.

144. Yardi, R. (1972), *A Study of the Differences in the pattern of Socialization of Rural Boys and Girls in Selected Village Near Delhi.* Lady Irwin College, Delhi University.

145. Yarrow, M.R. Scott, P.W. & Waxler, C.L. (1973), "Learning concern for others", *Developmental Psychology*, 55: 300-11.

146. Zameen, G.S. (1982), "A study of social, religious and moral values of students of class XI and their relationship with moral character traits and personality adjustment", *Fourth survey of Research in Education*, Buch, M.B.

147. Zimmerman, C.C. (1747), *Family and Civilization*, Harper, p. 827.

148. Zucker, H. (1943), "The emotional attachment of children to their parents as related to standards of behaviour and delinquency", *The Journal of Delinquency*, 44, 31-40.

INDEX

A

B

C

D

E

F

G

H

I

J

K

L

M

T

U

W

Y

Z